Continental L
Jim Hill - Zero

Jim Hill

To Johanna and Bob

I have always appreciated your
interest in my hikes - and
your trail magic, too. (Hint, Hint)

Jim

Cover Design by Karin Curtis-Hill
Edited by Johanna Smethurst

DEDICATION

To Nancy and John Pryor whose kind spirits, inquisitive minds, and zest for adventure are an inspiration to all who love them and to their loving family: John, Sharon, Aaron, Tad, and Francis.

This book tells about my Continental Divide Trail hike to the best of my memory.

Contents

1 CRAZY COOK

I thru-hiked the Appalachian Trail at age sixty-two and the Pacific Crest Trail at sixty-five. They were two of the most enjoyable adventures of my life. By the time I finished the Pacific Crest Trail I was pooped. I know I groused to anyone who would listen that my thru-hiking days were over but in the back of my mind a demanding drumbeat increased in intensity - triple crown, Triple Crown, TRIPLE CROWN! The Triple Crown is hiking the Appalachian Trail, Pacific Crest Trail, and Continental Divide Trail. The Continental Divide Trail is usually saved for last. It is only about 76% complete and there are times you create your own pathway around prairie dog holes, cactus, and thorny plants and bushes that are determined to stick you – and do. The distance of the Continental Divide Trail varies with the route you choose. It can be from 2,600 miles to over 3,100 miles. Since there are so many options for picking a route from Mexico to Canada, you really do "hike your own hike" through New Mexico, Colorado, Wyoming, a small part of Idaho, and Montana before finishing in Canada. I was now sixty-seven and in good health but there was a feeling I had better get this hike going and not push my luck.

My plan was to take the designated Continental Divide Trail by following Bear Creek's maps. If along the way there were Bear Creek alternate routes that were more spectacular, I would take them. I knew this was going to be the most challenging hike of all and I spent many more hours preparing for it. Most people start at an isolated monument in the dry, dusty desert called Crazy Cook. On May 4th 2014 I touched the monument and was on my way. What a great way to start a thru-hike! The Continental Divide Trail throws a lot at you all at once. I hope few changes are made to the Trail in the first 120 miles. If you have any deficiencies in planning, ability to navigate, physical fitness, or heart – they will be exploited. You will find out quickly you have to know what you are doing on the Continental Divide Trail.

My first goal was to hike eighty-five miles to Lordsburg, New Mexico in five days. There were hardly any natural water sources between Crazy Cook and Lordsburg so for a $10 fee, five metal water boxes holding gallon containers of water were provided at intervals within a day's walking distance. I wanted to stay well hydrated so I carried four, thirty-two ounce water bottles to make it to the first water cache fourteen miles away.

The Trail started on an actual pathway with CDT sign posts. Soon I was following a dilapidated dirt jeep road.

Creosote bushes were everywhere. Ocotillo plants were in bloom with their long thin branches topped by bright red flowers. The air was dry and even though it was hot, I was not sweating. I heard a rumble behind me that sounded like a jet and looked back to see a big column of swirling dust heading my way. A pathway formed of bushes being shaken violently and I grabbed my hat and hunched my shoulders to shield myself from the stinging sand. After a while my ears became attuned to the rumble of an approaching dust devil. They would come and go throughout the day.

The jeep road changed to cross country and I began to make my own pathway from rock cairn to rock cairn. I love bushwhacking! My brother, Doug, downloaded Bear Creek's maps onto my eTrex 30 GPS. The maps listed all the waypoints from Mexico to Canada and the rock cairns correlated with the waypoints. I would follow a GPS heading and be constantly scanning the horizon for a cairn to show up. It reminded me of an Easter egg hunt. It was fun when I would spot one in the distance – "Yes!" Once I was within a couple of hundred yards of it, a path would start to form. When I passed the cairn the pathway would gradually fade and I would again be dodging creosote bushes, cactus, rocks, and rabbit holes.

Water runoff from mountains to my west created countless arroyos along the desert floor. Crossing an arroyo, the footing was often unstable and my feet would slide on small rocks and loose soil. Some of the arroyos were deep enough that a fall could cause serious injury. I was alone and there was no one near to hear my calls for help so I would search back and forth along the edge looking for the safest way down. I was still not comfortable with my backpack and didn't yet have confidence in my balance. I depended heavily on my sturdy hickory hiking stick to keep from sliding out of control. I had a couple of minor falls that punctured my skin and a number of slides where I was expecting to fall and didn't and felt lucky.

I wore shorts and a short sleeved shirt which, in hind sight, wasn't the greatest idea. It seemed like all the plants and bushes had thorns. At times they were tightly spaced and I didn't have a choice but to work my way through them. By the time I reached Lordsburg my body looked like a pincushion. My nemesis was the jumping cholla cactus. Small spiny pieces about six inches long dropped from the main cactus and if I stepped too close, the vibration made them jump up and cling to my boots, socks, and skin. The barbs penetrated at different angles and when I tried to pull them off, some of the barbs penetrated even deeper. It took a lot of patience and a delicate touch to remove them.

I was expecting more of a flat desert which wasn't the case at all. In the course of a day I would hike through canyons, follow dirt roads steeply up and down along the base of mountains, wander cross country over rugged, rocky, cactus filled ground, travel through flat, arid ranch land, traverse a mind numbing number of arroyos, and hike beside hills right out of a Hollywood western where I could imagine a band of Apaches on horseback looking down on me from a ridge high above.

I crossed huge areas of sandy ranch land covered with creosote bushes, rabbit brush, cholla cactus, prickly pear cactus, barrel cactus, chamisa, and an occasional juniper or pinion tree. Southern New Mexico was experiencing a severe drought and it looked next to impossible for cattle to find enough to eat. I was surprised at how healthy they appeared. Miles of barbed wire enclosed the property of the ranches. I spent a lot of time climbing over it, sliding under it on my back, and gingerly sliding between the strands of wire trying not to snag my clothes. I had trouble with the barbed wire gates. Too many times the ranchers made them so tight it was hard to loosen the top loop of wire and it would spring loose and snag my skin. By Lordsburg, I had a rip on my shirt, my wind shirt, backpack, and numerous barbed wire gouges on my body. I fortunately remembered to get a tetanus shot before starting the hike.

My first day was spent trying to get into the rhythm of the hike. I wasn't in any hurry and planned to start slowly and listen closely to my body until I gained my trail legs. After all the preparation and anticipation, it felt good to finally be hiking. I was determined to take it easy. Going uphill, I intentionally slowed my pace. It was a bright, hot day and I was grateful for my sunscreen, shade hat, and sunglasses. My Keen Targhee II boots were well broken in and my Darn Tough socks and Dirty Girl gators were doing their job. Dirty Girl gators come in many eye catching patterns. Mine were lightning flashes against a deep blue background. Yee Haw!

Stopping for a break I tried to find a tree or an arroyo for shade. The few trees were pinion and juniper and surrounded by cow droppings. I would push away enough droppings for a place to sit and be grateful for the shade. The flies were incessant. While I was eating, I let them crawl on my body. As long as I didn't disturb them they would go about their business and be less of a nuisance. It probably looked strange having flies crawling over my body, but it worked for me. I didn't have much of an appetite and overestimated my food requirement which was going to leave me with a lot of extra food by the time I reached Lordsburg. It actually took me all the way to Silver City – fifty-eight miles up the Trail.

On the PCT I went stoveless relying heavily on a trail mix that I made myself. It did a great job of giving me the energy I needed but was hard, crunchy food, and I broke a tooth. For my CDT hike I also planned to go stoveless but try foods that were softer and easier to eat. Oatmeal and dehydrated pinto beans were my main staples. I used a plastic twenty-four ounce powdered Gatorade container to rehydrate them. Before going to bed I filled the container three-quarters of the way to the top with oatmeal, added raisins, Nido powdered milk, a pinch of cinnamon, and enough water to fill the container almost to the top. By morning the oatmeal was fully hydrated. It was a filling, good tasting breakfast that I never tired of.

After breakfast, I poured four ounces of water into the Gatorade container, tightened the lid, and shook the container to clean it. I drank whatever remained of the oatmeal, filled the container half way with dehydrated pinto beans, put in some Mrs. Dash seasoning, and added water three-quarters of the way to the top to allow for expansion of the beans. The beans took three hours to fully hydrate. They were loaded with complex carbohydrates for an even burn of energy, protein to rebuild and maintain muscle, and dense with calories for their weight. Throughout the day I alternated between pinto beans and oatmeal. I eat pinto beans practically every day at home and love them. I thought this would be a good fit. It wasn't. They tasted terrible! I was hoping my hiker appetite would eventually kick in, but in the mean time I could barely choke them down. The beans didn't get any better in the next four days to Lordsburg and I realized I was going to have to find a way to make them more appetizing.

I arrived at the first water box just as it was getting dark and I was tired. My body wasn't used to hiking eight hours with a pack. I set up my new tent for the first time and did a lousy job of it. I fixed my dinner, carried it over to a soft spot of sand, sat down, and leaned back against a smooth rock. It felt good to be off of my feet. It was starting to get chilly and the warmth of my wind shirt felt good, too. Living in a city, I am accustomed to being around constant sound. The desert was so quiet. As I ate my dinner under the stars, I felt that relaxed, peaceful feeling that I love.

The wind picked up just as I finished dinner and came on with a vengeance. My tent was loudly flapping throughout the night. I should have gone out and tightened it, but I didn't, and got very little sleep. At 3:00 am I heard a high pitched whistle that sounded like my brand new Therm-a-Rest Neo Air mattress deflating. Great! Just Great! The mattress didn't feel like it was deflating. I blew it up even tighter. It continued to intermittently whistle. I finally realized the lid on one of my water bottles hadn't been tightened enough and the air pressure from the 4,400 foot altitude caused the air inside of the bottle to slowly leak.

The next morning I was groggy from lack of sleep and my stomach was still complaining about the beans from the day before. Flies were buzzing incessantly. I was tired and grumpy and they really bugged me. It took all day to hike twelve miles to the next water box. Twelve lethargic miles. I arrived at the water box at 7:00 pm, set up my tent, had some dinner, and was asleep by 8:00 pm. I slept eleven straight hours.

The morning started with a cross country climb. I passed an abandoned mine that didn't go down more than about twenty feet, but it filled me with a feeling of a time long past. Over a hundred years ago there was a miner digging this hole hoping to "strike it rich". I could almost see him drenched in sweat as he toiled away with his pick and shovel.

Heading north the Little Hatchet Mountains were to my west for most of the day. There were limitless vistas ahead. Looking back I could still see the huge Mormon farm co-ops in Mexico. Far on the horizon were towering dust devils. My boots crunched over uneven sand and rocks as I maneuvered around cactus, clumps of dry grass, thorny plants, and creosote bushes. A gentle breeze kept the flies away and felt good on my sunburned skin. Crows soared on thermals and without competition from other sounds their aggressive calls were surprisingly loud – CAW, CAW, CAW! I made it to the third water cache in the afternoon and called it a day. I was pleasantly tired. I was in no hurry. I wanted to give the snow in the San Juan Mountains of Southern Colorado plenty of time to melt.

It was cool and windy as I began the fourth day. After a couple of hours I took a break. I dropped down into a small arroyo about five feet deep and eight feet wide with a steep embankment that provided good protection from the wind. I sat down and worked my way into the sandy soil until I was almost in a reclining position. I was perfectly relaxed as I looked up at white fluffy clouds floating lazily across a bright blue sky. I closed my eyes, felt the warmth of the sun on my body, and fell into a peaceful sleep. I heard a sound and opened my eyes. On the edge of the arroyo, looming above me was a hiker! What a pleasant surprise! I hadn't seen a hiker in four days. I quickly packed up and joined him. His trail name was Argentina. He was tall and wiry and it would have looked comical seeing us hiking together. I took two steps to each one of his long loping strides. We hiked and talked for the next three hours. My guess is that he was in his early fifties. The first thing I noticed was that his back was out of alignment. He told me major surgery hadn't helped and he lived with constant back pain. Watching him was like getting a lesson in the meaning of the word - determination. I could see that he really did live in pain. It was hard watching him trying to negotiate barbed wire. I wanted to help. He ate his food lying on his back. Once in a while he would stop hiking and lean his full weight on his hiking poles to take the pressure off of his back. We took a break in the shade of water box #4. Argentina had Bear Creek's maps downloaded to his eTrex 20 GPS but was unable to access the waypoints. I took a look at his GPS to see if I could figure it out. Unfortunately, I couldn't. In the meantime he was using his compass and maps for navigation. He was trying to catch up to a group of friends who were four days ahead and he was much faster than me so I let him go on his way. He was one tough, determined man and I had nothing but admiration for him.

I spent the rest of the day bushwhacking through barren, windswept, range land. Sometimes I would come across Argentina's size 13 Cascadia 7 shoe prints. I was using my GPS heading from cairn to cairn. All I had to do was keep the arrow pointing at the waypoint. Argentina was using his map and compass. It was really irritating to see that he was navigating a more direct course to each cairn. After a while I was grumbling to myself: "Damned overachiever!" I followed Argentina's footprints all the way to northern New Mexico.

This was arid ranch land. I passed tractor tires filled with water for the cattle. The water looked pretty good. I would definitely have used it if I had needed it. I stopped at 7:00 pm and found a smooth spot on a sandy knoll to put my tent. It was very windy so I used all the tie-downs and staked my Big Agnes Seedhouse SL1 tent extra tight. The gusty wind absolutely pounded the tent all through the night. It was so loud my sleep was erratic, but I had peace of mind knowing my tent would hold. I have used the SL1 on the AT, PCT, and CDT and never encountered a wind storm or thunderstorm it couldn't handle - and I have encountered some memorable ones.

The next morning I hiked through this vast, flat, dry,

lonely, land for twelve miles before finally reaching some hills. It felt good to be hiking up and down winding ranch roads again. I could see a windmill in the distance surrounded by shady trees. Great! The perfect place to take a break! As I got closer I could see twenty cows and one big bull had the same idea. The road I was walking on took me to within fifteen feet of the bull. His eyes locked onto mine. I picked up my pace and began to whistle softly and hopefully - soothingly. I was also trying to figure out where I would run if he charged. I made it past but continued to glance back just to make sure he hadn't changed his mind.

In the afternoon I took a break in the shade of the fifth water box. I couldn't be more grateful to the people who kept those water boxes stocked. They were truly life savers. The next four miles to my camping spot was rugged, rocky, hilly, cross country hiking. After a twenty-one mile day I was one weary hiker and was sound asleep five minutes after getting into my sleeping bag.

The next morning I was raring to go. It was only four miles to Lordsburg where I planned to spend the night at the Econo Lodge. I could see Lordsburg in the distance and instead of following the Bear Creek waypoints I started making a beeline for the heart of town. Big mistake! Steep hills, deep canyons, and arroyos had me scrambling. At one time I was actually searching for handholds and footholds to get up the side of a canyon. I could see Lordsburg and it looked so close! I stubbornly continued scrambling. After way too long I came to the conclusion: "Get your dumb ass back on the Trail!" I was so far off course it took a lot of effort just to get back to the Trail. I was pissed. A hot shower, clean bed, and good food were calling so I didn't stay pissed for long. I reached the Econo Lodge by 11:00 am and they were kind enough to give me a room right away.

Water in the desert is scarce and used for hydration, not cleaning. After five days I was funky. Taking a shower was a luxury. I shaved, brushed my teeth, and felt half-way human again. I was starving, though, and there was a Kranberry's Restaurant right across the street. It was a chain restaurant whose main customers were Interstate 10 travelers. I love Mexican food and was looking forward to a big burrito. I had a feeling it was going to be bland so it wouldn't startle the taste buds of non-New Mexicans. When the burrito arrived at the table it was hiker sized, spicy and delicious! I hadn't had much of an appetite for the last five days and I devoured it. I headed back to the Econo Lodge. What a great, hiker friendly motel! The manager and all the employees went out of their way to make me feel welcome. This is where the shuttle arrived each morning to pick up thru-hikers to take them to Crazy Cook. The Econo Lodge had an excellent discount for thru-hikers. There was a free breakfast with a good selection of food including do it yourself waffles. They even cleaned my hiking clothes for free and dried them separately from the regular laundry so they wouldn't wrinkle. I should have offered a five dollar tip because of the money, time, and effort they saved me but I didn't think of it at the time and regretted it afterwards. On my thru-hikes I have noticed when motel owners, or their staff, go out of their way to be kind and helpful it leaves me with a good memory - not just of my pleasant stay at the motel - but of the town. Lordsburg was out in the middle of the desert with a population of about 4,000 people. The downtown was peppered with boarded up former businesses, its best years were far in the past, yet I smile each time I think of that welcoming little town.

After a refreshing sleep I was ready to head the fifty-eight miles to Silver City. The first water source listed on the Bear Creek map was fourteen miles away. To make sure I started the day well hydrated, I had a glass of orange juice and four cups of coffee with breakfast. Bad decision! The CDT went through the heart of town, then four more miles on Highway 70 and Highway 90 before heading cross country. I dawdled along checking out the town and stopping at the grocery store to pick up some ketchup for the beans. I was riding a nice caffeine high heading out of town. After about a mile, the four cups of coffee started making their presence known. Highway 70 had a lot of traffic and there were no trees or culverts for privacy. By mile three I was hiking at over four miles an hour, clicking my teeth, and in desperate need of relief. I was giving myself a pep talk that was beginning to collide with reality.

"It's less than a mile to the cross country turn-off. I can make it."

"I'm not going to make it. This is going to be humiliating when I start taking a pee right next to the road with cars passing in both directions. I can't hold it much longer."

Highway 90 veered to the right and $3/10^{th}$ of a mile in the distance was the cross country turn-off. I started to jog. I made it to the fence, quickly slid under the barbed wire, and made it thirty yards up the Trail before I couldn't go any further. Aahh! Sweet relief!

I began a gradual nine mile climb that started at 4,222' and reached 5,400' by the first designated water source. Near an arroyo I passed the sun bleached bones of a dead cow. It was the first of many dead animals I encountered in this harsh, unforgiving desert. By the sixth day of hiking my mind was automatically finding the most efficient course to take around creosote bushes, cactus, rocks, small plants, clumps of grass, and prairie dog holes. Animal holes were everywhere. Some were big enough that a wrong step could easily twist an ankle or break a leg. I had close calls where I narrowly averted stepping into a hole at the last moment. Sometimes I would step on the edge of a hole, start sliding in, and quickly make a correction. The thought of a hike ending twisted ankle kept me constantly scanning the ground.

I reached the first water source in the afternoon. It was a metal tube in the ground about two feet wide and three feet deep. There was a float to regulate the flow of water. I tried to get it to work but it had been shut down by the rancher who owned the property. New Mexico was in a bad drought and ranchers were not running cattle on land that they normally would. I started with four quarts of water and was shepherding my water just in case something like this happened, but I only had a quart of water left. The next water was 7/10th of a mile further. I had written on my map: "This tank should be better." It was also a metal tube in the ground with a float valve and as dry as the first one! There was a big water storage tank nearby. I climbed the ladder to the top and looked in. Dry as a bone! Yikes! On my map I had written: "Next water 23 miles." Yikes again! In fact, this was scary! I had a little less than a quart of water to make it twenty-three miles to Mud Springs in the hot, dry, desert. Twenty-three miles was doable but I would be hurting badly. The thing that kept running through my mind and causing HUGE anxiety was: "What if Mud Springs is dry?" I resigned myself to conserving my energy and slowly grinding out the twenty-three miles to Mud Springs. I planned to keep hiking into the cooler temperatures of the night, relying heavily on my GPS to stay oriented. There was an Engineers Windmill listed in one mile but it wasn't designated as a WT source on the Bear Creek map. I had seen a number of windmills that were missing parts and hadn't been used in years and I wasn't optimistic. I could see the top of the windmill in the distance. It was slanted at an angle and missing blades. Shit! As I got closer I heard an unexpected sound. Could that be splashing water? I turned the corner, saw cattle resting under a shady tree, and a ten foot high tank with water cascading over the top. A solar well! What a gorgeous sight! What a gorgeous sound! I drank two quarts right on the spot and filled my four water bottles as the cold refreshing water splashed on my body. Heaven!

I reached Mud Springs the following afternoon. I was down to a quart of water and even more grateful for the water at the Engineers Windmill. Mud Springs had character. It was in a shaded area slightly off of the Trail. I had a feeling this had been the water source of living creatures for thousands of years. I felt honored to be using it. The spring was a hole in the ground about five feet in diameter. It looked fairly deep. The water was cool to the touch and more green than blue. The surface was covered with green slime and dead bugs. It looked great! I used my Sawyer filter for the first time. It was surprisingly quick and worked like a champ! Soon I had four quarts of clean, sparkling water. (When I cleaned the filter at the motel in Silver City the next day I was amazed at the quantity of green gunk it had filtered.) The Trail was clearly defined in this area and I hiked another couple of miles before calling it a day. After twenty-two miles on a hot windy day, I was tired. It was eighteen miles to Silver City and I was looking forward to another motel break.

Before heading out the next morning, I turned on my GPS and checked my map. Something wasn't right. According to the map, I should have been on a road. Instead, I was on a dirt pathway camped right next to a CDT sign. My GPS didn't show any waypoints ahead. It showed the last waypoint to be almost all the way back at Mud Springs. I didn't want to hike back over the same area just to re-orient with my GPS so I decided to take the clearly marked Trail. Dumb! Really Dumb! Of course the Trail I was following wasn't marked on my map, but I reassured myself it was only 18 miles to Silver City and I was heading in the right direction. It was a beautiful wide pathway with lots of shady trees and excellent views. I patted myself on the back. What an excellent decision! Around the six mile mark I saw my last CDT sign. The Trail began to fizzle and eventually ended. I looked all over the place for any semblance of a trail -

nothing. I saw a small ranch road three hundred yards downhill and bushwhacked to it. I don't remember being overly upset. After hiking the Appalachian Trail and Pacific Crest Trail I had learned to "go with the flow". Sometimes I make good decisions - sometimes not so good. It wasn't the end of the world. There was no use trying to salvage the hike the rest of the way to Silver City – I no longer had a Trail to follow - so I planned to hitch a ride if I was fortunate enough to get one. Since I live in New Mexico, I knew I would come back and finish this section at the completion of my CDT thru-hike. I headed down the small dirt road hoping it would eventually meet up with the nearest highway. After about a mile I looked back and saw a king cab pickup truck heading my way. It was a pleasure to see it slow down and stop. The driver was in his forties. The guy in the front seat was in his mid-twenties as was the guy in the back seat.

"You need a ride?"

"You Bet!"

"Hop in. Where are you heading?"

"Silver City." I hopped in.

"Silver City is fifty miles from here."

I didn't say anything but I was thinking….."That was a strange answer. Something isn't quite right. Be careful. Don't say or do anything to antagonize them. Keep your answers short and positive. Appear relaxed and grateful for the ride."

I glanced at the man sitting next to me. There was tin foil coming out of the bottom of his trousers, his long sleeved shirt, and his collar. He introduced himself as

"Pluto". Great!

It was the young man in the front seat that had me worried. He was asking a lot of questions and seemed the most the sensitive to my answers.

I let them do most of the talking and answered their questions cheerfully and positively.

After about ten minutes the young man in the front seat lifted the newspaper in his lap and underneath was the biggest pistol I have seen in my life! He put the pistol into the glove compartment.

"We're heading to Silver City, too. I was jokin' about the fifty miles. Where are you staying?"

"The Motel 6."

"We'll drop you off."

"Thanks. I appreciate it."

I looked relaxed but I stayed totally focused until they dropped me off.

I checked into the Motel 6, had a long refreshing shower, shaved, brushed my teeth, and took a nap. There was a Taco Bell nearby and I headed to it. I ordered two of the biggest burritos on the menu. My hiker appetite had arrived. Back at the motel, I called my sister, Johanna, and brother, Doug. I don't carry a phone while hiking so once I stop at a motel I give them a call. We have an agreement that I will call them at least once every two weeks while thru-hiking and it is always a pleasure getting caught up. I called my cousin Deborah and her husband Dan to give them an update on my progress. Deborah and Dan were staying at my house and taking care of my beagle, Fred. They mentioned a fire just outside of Silver City. When I checked into the motel, I noticed a news van from one of the Albuquerque TV stations parked in the motel parking lot. On the drive to Silver City I had seen a big plume of smoke that looked like it was in the area where I would be hiking the next day. It was causing anxiety.

There was another thing that was causing anxiety. I needed a better plan for dealing with the water in the desert. I tried to imagine what it would have been like if there hadn't been water at the Engineers Windmill. It didn't take much imagination to know I would have been in a world of hurt! I remembered the sinking feeling in the pit of my stomach when I realized I would have to hike twenty-three miles on less than a quart of water. My new plan was to make sure I always took enough water to pass two of the designated WT sources on Bear Creek's maps and be able to make it to the third. Any time I found water I would camel up and fill back up to four quarts. I was hiking in drought conditions and I had to be prepared for water sources being dry. I didn't like the idea of the extra weight but I wasn't going to be a gram wienie when it came to water.

2 GILA RIVER

The next morning I stopped at the grocery store and bought enough food to make it forty-five miles to my next resupply box at Doc Campbell's Store. I followed the CDT through Silver City and picked up the Walnut Creek alternate route leaving town. There was a big plume of smoke in the distance and I could smell it. I was dreading a fire closure but decided to keep hiking and take my chances. Much to my relief the Trail started to gradually veer away from the fire. After seven miles I reached the start of the Bear Creek Gila River alternate trail. The regular Continental Divide Trail met here, too. Someone had thoughtfully left five containers of water for hikers and I filled up. I was really looking forward to the Gila River section. The 105 mile Gila River alternate route was supposed to be spectacular. I would be crossing the Gila River over 200 times.

After a short break I started hiking what I thought was the Gila River alternate. I hiked along a wide pathway for a half-mile before checking my GPS. The arrow to the next waypoint pointed to the right. I continued on, thinking the pathway would probably swing to the right and the arrow would make the proper correction. The pathway gradually veered to the left and the arrow swung further to the right. My bright conclusion: "There must be something wrong with the GPS." I hiked another half-mile before my stubborn mind finally relented and decided to trust the GPS and follow the arrow to the waypoint. I did some heavy duty bushwhacking, and cussing, before getting back on course.

My body was recharged after a good night's sleep and lots of food in Silver City and I had energy to spare. I was losing the aches, hot spots, and chafing associated with the first few days of a hike and beginning to get my Trail legs. It felt good to work up a sweat. I hiked up and down mountains and through deep canyons. I passed lichen covered boulders and dead trees with gnarled branches that formed beautiful silhouettes against the blue sky. Tight straw colored grass covered the ground with long strands flowing in the breeze. Cactus, creosote bushes, juniper, and pinion were in abundance; even tall pines started to show up for the first time. There were terrific views and shady spots to take a break and enjoy them. On climbs, my lungs struggled for air and I would take in as much oxygen as possible. I probably sounded like the "little train that could", huffing and puffing my way up the mountain but I know it gave me extra energy. Once the Trail levelled, my respiration and heartrate would automatically recover. This happened dozens of times a day and created an incredibly efficient cardio-vascular system - one of the perks of thru-hiking.

In the afternoon walking along the canyon floor I saw a rattlesnake five feet to my right. I was already past the ornery bugger when it started to rattle at me. The intensity of its rattle went from zero to one hundred in about one second. My arms were immediately covered with goose bumps and the hair on the back of my neck and arms stood on end! That is a truly frightening sound and the animal reaction to it is automatic, instinctive, and immediate.

For the past few hours I had seen bear droppings on the Trail. I hiked into the evening hoping to get out of its territory. As I was putting up my tent I noticed at least eight droppings within fifty feet. Before going to sleep I double bagged my food and put the food bag into a plastic sack with my toothpaste, sun tan lotion, and anything else with an odor. I closed the plastic sack, tied the top, put it into my backpack and covered the pack with my hiking clothes. Once I was in my sleeping bag I started listening for sounds in the night. I was tired. I needed sleep. After a while I said: "Screw it! If a bear comes after my food I will deal with it when it happens." I fell into a deep sleep and slept through the night. I awoke the next morning feeling lucky nothing had happened.

I wonder if I would have even heard a bear. When I first start a thru-hike, my sleep is restless and I hear sounds I am not used to. By the time I get my trail legs, which takes about ten days, I also start to sleep soundly. My body is weary from hiking ten solid hours and ready for rejuvenating sleep. I never wear earplugs because the sounds of crickets, leaves rustling in the breeze, or a gently flowing stream, relax me and help me fall asleep. I also don't wear earplugs because I want to hear potential sounds of danger. I feel so at ease in the forest and settle into such a deep sleep, I wonder how many of those potential sounds of danger I have slept through.

I hiked a couple of hours in the morning before catching the first glimpse of the Gila River. It was far below and took a couple of hours on the steep switch backed Trail to reach it. While hiking the Continental Divide Trail I had seen few hikers – not just thru-hikers but any hikers. I would sing and talk to myself knowing no one was around. As I was descending I really ripped a fart. I turned a corner and two teen aged girls were heading toward me only twenty feet away. I was embarrassed. One of the girls acted offended. The other was having a hard time suppressing a giggle. I nodded and kept going. When I reached the river the first thing I noticed was the soothing sound of smoothly flowing water. After the parched desert, I stood still and savored it. Soon I was ready to make my first ford. I was excited! I lost my balance as I worked my way down a muddy embankment and it took a spectacular save with my hiking stick to keep from falling flat into the water. I was thinking: "What a start! I've got 200 more of these?" I was expecting the water to be cold and it wasn't. Pleasant would be the best word to describe it. I picked the shallowest area and waded across. The water stayed below my knees. It was fun! One down!

The Gila River is in a canyon that expands and contracts creating islands between the canyon walls and the river. A huge flood had ravaged the area the previous fall. One of the first things I noticed on the islands were all the downed trees, uprooted bushes, broken branches, and every imaginable kind of debris piled against trees, rocks, boulders, logs, stumps, and anything strong enough to impede their forward progress. There had been a defined pathway before the flood; now much of that was gone.

I am going to take you with me on my first day hiking along the Gila River. Pretend you are a Go Pro camera attached to my forehead. Be prepared for soggy boots and socks because I am not taking them off.

Walking along the river the sound of flowing water is a pleasant constant. On my right is a towering canyon wall. I am walking over small rocks and sand on a beach between the wall and the river. The river meets the canyon wall and my pathway fizzles out. I look for a place to cross. I see deep pools. To my left the water sparkles as it flows rapidly over small rocks. This looks like my best bet. I feel the pull of the current as I head across. It is an easy crossing. I make my way out of the river onto a twenty foot wide beach made up of rounded river rocks. The uneven rocks extend for three hundred yards along the side of the river. I have to carefully watch where I step so I don't sprain an ankle. I am looking for the pathway on this side of the canyon. I finally see it and scramble up a five foot embankment to get to it. The well-worn pathway veers away from the river and takes me through a shady area thick with oak trees and covered with vegetation. After a couple of hundred yards the pathway spits me back out at the river. I walk on river rocks for a while, then on a wide sandy beach. There is a lot of debris from the flood in this area. I have to work my way around and sometimes over it. I lose any semblance of a trail. Fifty yards ahead the beach and river meet at a steep canyon wall. The river is thirty feet wide with a swift flow. I don't see any easy crossing choices. I step into the water and it is immediately above my knees. The water tries to take control and I rely heavily on my hiking stick to stay balanced. There are big rocks next to an area that looks to be fairly shallow. I head in that direction. The water is now up to my shorts. I walk over uneven rocks covered with slippery moss. My right foot slides on the slick moss. I jam my hiking stick down. Fortunately it finds a good spot and holds. Close call! My adrenaline is pumping! I make it to the shallow area. The water is now at my knees. It's a warm day and the cool water feels good. I splash around just for the fun of it as I work my way to the far bank. I search for a pathway but it has been completely washed out. The grass, smaller plants, and bushes are matted down and still flow in the direction of the flood. Debris clings to trees. Some of it is above my head. I come to a downed tree with thick, tangled branches that block my forward progress. I see a way through but I will have to climb over wobbly branches to get there. As I get higher off the ground the branches become even more wobbly. I am now five feet above the ground. All that is left is to step on a small branch and use it to spring over. It doesn't look very sturdy. I could head back down and try to find another way through but I've worked hard to get this far. All I have to do is step on that branch and spring over. It sure looks puny......Naw! It's sturdy enough! I put my full weight on the branch and hear a sickening "CRACK!" Shit! I am off balance and grab onto anything to break my fall. I land on my feet but my right arm hits a branch and tears open a good sized chunk of skin. It starts to bleed heavily. I head over to the river, wash the wound, cover it with Neosporin, put on a bandage, and head on my way.

This is hard hiking. It is humid and I am sweating profusely. Flies are buzzing around attempting to land on me and their constant buzzing is annoying. I am dodging plants, bushes, stacked up piles of debris, clumps of grass, and big ruts in the ground. I'm kicking up dust, my legs are filthy, and I've got a banged up arm. Poor Jim! It's a fine time for a pity party! I indulge.

The pity party doesn't last long. The river swings around a

bend and opens to a lovely setting. I decide to take a break. I sit down and lean back against a big shady cottonwood tree. Just in front of me is a large pool of still water with an almost perfect reflection of the nearby trees and canyon wall. On my right is the deeply eroded canyon wall. Plants grow from its base with branches that gracefully flow down to the water. Across the river I see a sandy beach and an island full of cottonwoods. As I enjoy my lunch I hear water trickling over a rocky shoal. I inhale the pleasant, subtle fragrance of the cottonwood's leaves. A bird is singing his heart out trying to attract a mate. He sings an intricate, trilling song. I try to imitate his song and fail miserably. I am completely relaxed. Life is good.

After my break, I cross the river and find a well-used pathway. I am grateful because there is flood debris everywhere. I see a ripped up sleeping bag snagged on an uprooted tree. I see the side of a mobile home wedged between trees. I have seen a number of remnants of mobile homes. This must have been one hellacious flood. The pathway leads back to the river. A horseback rider holding onto the reins of a pack horse is crossing the river and heading my way. Four extremely fit mongrel dogs are charging back and forth across the water, barking, and having the time of their lives. The current is strong and the horses make easy work of it as they loudly splash across. Once across, the rider notices me watching him. He almost jumps out of his saddle. I understand his reaction. It is rare to see another person on the Continental Divide Trail. We exchange greetings and he heads down the Trail. The horses make the crossing look easy so I attempt the same crossing. That lasts about ten seconds before I go to Plan B.

The canyon narrows. The walls are sheer and steep on both sides. I see a pathway that heads away from the wall and up the side of the mountain. My map shows it will meet back with the river in a quarter of a mile. The river is not deep in this area and the walls only extend a hundred yards until I can get back on land. I decide to walk the river. It is shallow and there is very little current so I won't have to concentrate on staying upright. I admire the towering, deeply eroded sandstone walls. I am splashing along enjoying myself and the next instant I'm flat on my back with water flowing around me. It is immediate and stunning! My clothes are soaked. My backpack is soaked. Everything on the inside of my backpack is enclosed in a heavy duty garbage bag. My GPS, camera, wallet, and maps are enclosed in zip lock bags so the only damage is to my pride. I decide not to press my luck and head back to the overland route.

The next hours are filled with many river crossings. I am getting better at finding the best crossings and using my hiking stick more effectively. I find a stable place to plant my stick, lean on it as I work my way forward, stop, find another stable place to plant my stick and continue forward. Often there are islands on both sides of the river. I am constantly trying to decide which island has the easiest route to follow. My eyes are scanning across the river for signs of a pathway or at least less foliage and debris to travel through. It is uncanny the number of times I head across the river and up an embankment and meet up with Argentina's shoe prints. Even in areas where we have to bushwhack, there are Argentina's shoe prints and no others. It's like our minds are making the same decisions, out of a myriad of options, to find the most efficient course along the river.

The canyon narrows until the nearly vertical walls are thirty feet apart. Unless I want to take a long detour, my only option is to take the Trail up a fifty foot canyon wall. As I head up, the Trail becomes more challenging. By the time I near the top I am climbing in places. The drop-off is fifty feet down and it has my undivided attention. It is decision time. I'm not confident of the foot hold and hand holds that will get me past the last remaining obstacle. Should I go back down and take the safer route? It's probably my best bet. There is no hurry. I've got all the time in the world. If I fall my hike is over. I need to chill out for a few minutes to assess the situation. While I'm chilling I check the obstacle. Can I get a good hand grip and foothold that would give me enough stability? Let me try the handhold right there. Yea, that works. Now I'll put my left foot right here. My balance is good. It feels stable. Now my other hand right here. One more step and I've got it made. Don't look down. Made it!

It's now evening. I have crossed the Gila River over thirty times and I'm ready to find a place to camp. I see a beautiful location about twenty yards from the Trail nestled in the shade of ponderosa pines. I have to climb over a downed tree to get there. When I reach the spot I am startled to see a young couple sitting next to their tent. I can tell immediately they are not thru-hikers. They both give me a nod of greeting. I see disappointment in the woman's eyes. I sense she has a memorable evening planned. I turn around and head back to the Trail. Not one word is exchanged but so much is said.

I hate to bring your day to an abrupt end, but I can't remember where I camped. I vividly remember the next two nights and can recall every camping spot from day one, but I can't bring back that first night camping beside the Gila River for the life of me.

I started hiking early the next morning. My hiker appetite was in full force and all I could think about was reaching Doc Campbell's and stuffing my face with food. Doc Campbell's is a small store along the road to the Gila National Monument. It caters to tourists and nearby ranchers and is very convenient for thru-hikers. I reached Doc Campbell's by 10:00 am and purchased and microwaved a beef burrito, bean and cheese burrito, and a really good breakfast burrito. Doc Campbell's is known for its homemade ice cream. I had a big tub of chocolate ice cream and a big tub of coffee flavored ice cream. It didn't disappoint. When I finished eating, I picked up my two resupply boxes and took them out to a picnic table in front of the store. I don't know what I was thinking when I made up those boxes. I still only needed one pound of food a day while hiking, and including the food that was in my pack, I now had twenty-two pounds! That was enough food to make it ninety-two miles to Reserve, forty miles to Pie Town, and seventy-five miles to Grants with food to spare. I couldn't forward the extra food from Doc Campbell's which meant I would have to put pounds of good food into the hiker box and I just couldn't do it. It took an hour to organize everything and stuff it into my backpack. My backpack looked like it would explode if you popped it with a needle. I was stressed. I needed a beef and bean burrito plus a large cup of coffee with extra cream and sugar to relieve that stress. Yea! Much better! It was noon by the time I left Doc Campbell's. I felt like a disgruntled packhorse heading back to the Trail with my 37 pound pack. I started increasing my food consumption just to get rid of the extra weight. One benefit – I had energy to spare.

I was riding a pig-out-high the rest of the extremely enjoyable day. I passed stately sycamore trees with their leaves gently shimmering in the breeze. Unlike most trees that head straight up to the sunlight, the sycamores seem to gracefully meander any way they please. I added them to my list of favorite trees. Further along I came upon sandstone canyon walls unlike anything I had ever seen. They were at least fifty feet high and in columns. Over the ages the weather had formed them into fantastic shapes. Looking at the rock formations, if I used my imagination, I could see elves, imps, and gargoyle faces. I later heard them described as hoodoos.

I hiked through a quarter mile section hit especially hard by the flood. The area was clogged with bushes, broken branches, and all kinds of small and large debris. Downed trees were stacked on top of one another or leaning against standing trees. Uprooted trees still containing all of their branches had crashed into thick bushes. Tightly spaced trees acted as a barrier to pile this mess together and I had to get through it. It reminded me of the decision making that went into navigating the boulder-filled Mahoosuc Notch on the Appalachian Trail. It was very physical. I was pushing through bushes and branches and climbing over or sliding under fallen trees. I would get into situations where I could make it through with a bold move but would pay the price if I failed. There is nothing like the element of danger to keep you focused and totally in the moment. I had a blast!

By 8:00 pm I made it to the intersection of Little Bear Canyon and the Middle Fork of the Gila River. I was in a narrow box canyon with vertical walls towering more than a hundred feet high. There was a fire ring surrounded by logs and an area for tents on smooth well-worn ground. I set up my tent with just the netting; then made some dinner. I took my dinner over to the fire ring, sat down, and leaned back against one of the big logs. I was completely relaxed after a fun day of hiking. As I ate my dinner I gazed up through tall ponderosa pines at stars that seemed to touch the tree tops. The smoothly flowing Gila River provided gentle background music. Five star dining under the stars.

I know I earlier described the water temperature as pleasant. That is not entirely accurate. It was cold the next morning when I began my hike. The first river crossing was in a part of the canyon yet to be hit by the morning sun. I winced when the iced cold water crept to the bottom of my shorts. As I kept moving forward I felt its icy tentacles slowly inching up my shorts. My mind was begging: "Please! No further!" The damned river wasn't sympathetic to my plea.

This was a day of narrow canyons and gorgeous scenery. I couldn't wait to follow the next bend in the river and see what beauty lay ahead. I was nearing the end of my hike along the Gila River. It had been fun but I was ready for those river crossings to end. I camped the last night two miles before Snow Lake on a sandy beach right next to the river. By 8:30 pm I was in my sleeping bag and heard people approaching my tent. It turned out to be Walker and Medic. I met them in Lordsburg at breakfast at the Econo Lodge. They were planning to night hike to Snow Lake. I never did actually see them. I was in my sleeping bag so I talked with them through my tent. We chatted for a few minutes before they headed on.

I had been hiking the Continental Divide Trail for fifteen days and had hiked 236 miles. In that time, the only thru-hiker I had actually seen while hiking was Argentina. Did I feel lonely? Not in the least! The Trail was providing ample entertainment.

The Gila River hike stayed beautiful right to the end. On my map was a notation: "Spigot at Snow Lake campground." I had put the same notation next to a campground just outside of Silver City and hadn't found water. With the river I had a sure thing. I filled up with clear, clean river water. It was a pleasure not having to carry water while hiking along the Gila River. Now I was carrying four quarts which weighed nine pounds, twenty pounds of food, and a fifteen pound base weight. I was carrying Forty-Four Freaking Pounds! Ugh! I could feel it.

I reached Snow Lake by 10:00 am. It had a nice campground and was bigger than I expected. I had the whole place to myself. May 19th was probably too early for vacationers. Leaving Snow Lake I followed a road for three miles before it branched left and I headed cross country. I stopped for a food break, sat down, and leaned back against an old shady ponderosa pine. I could smell the wonderful vanilla/pine aroma that only ponderosas give off. Cows were grazing in a nearby field. I felt completely relaxed – almost lazy. After I finished eating I closed my eyes, took a short nap, and woke up refreshed. I followed a barren canyon for a couple of miles; then made a steep climb to the top of an 8,000 foot mountain and onto a huge plain. I was the highest object for miles around. Getting caught in a thunderstorm in this area would have been terrifying. After the steep climb I was ready for a break. I took out my food bag and placed a water bottle within arm's reach. Oatmeal, Nido Powdered Milk, raisins, and cinnamon had been hydrating in my Gatorade container for the past two hours. I slid my backpack behind me, sat down on soft sandy soil between clumps of grass, and leaned back against the bottom of the pack. As I ate my food I was looking at fenceless dry grassland for as far as I could see. It was only 3:00 pm which was too early to camp. I was disappointed. I was on top of a mountain in a vast wide open space. I rarely cowboy camp but this would have been the perfect time. I could imagine waking up in the night, resting my hands behind my head, and from the warmth of my sleeping bag, gazing at a sky covered with stars - like being in a real life planetarium with stars extending all the way to the ground on all sides.

After my break I walked along a rutted dirt road for five miles before finally reaching some trees. It was late evening before I called it a day – a satisfying day. I heard coyotes howling in the night. I love that sound. It tells me I'm away from civilization and part of nature. Someday I would love to hear wolves making their mournful calls in the night. Coyotes were howling early the next morning, too. It was chilly and I wasn't in any hurry to get up so I rolled over and slept an extra hour. I finally started hiking at 9:00 am and followed the road through the forest for a half mile before it opened onto another huge plain. The road headed northeast for a mile then turned sharply northwest where it travelled in a straight line for an ungodly distance. Within minutes a car stopped and a young woman asked if I needed a ride. I said no and she smiled, shrugged, and took off. It was kind of depressing watching that car get tinier and tinier until it was just a miniscule dust trail before entering the forest.

This was fenced ranchland dotted with cattle tanks and much different than the grassland I hiked through the day before. Pickup trucks were coming and going as ranchers tended to their cattle. After three hours I reached the forest.

The road continued on a relatively straight line for another mile and a half as it gradually increased in elevation. It was rewarding looking back through the trees and seeing where I had started hours ago. The road followed Cox Canyon for the next four miles through a fragrant pine forest. Eventually it left the canyon and swung northwest. I was starting to get low on water and had circled Dutchman Tank on my map with the notation "should have water". I could see the manmade tank in the distance. A pickup truck stopped and a kind rancher asked if I needed water. I looked in the back of his truck to see if he had a water container and he didn't. I planned to camel up plus fill four quart bottles with water. I didn't want to short him so I said no. When I reached the Dutchman Tank and saw its water, I was kicking myself.

Cattle resting under shady trees ignored me as I prepared to get water from the tank. It was twenty feet in diameter. The entrance was surrounded by mud and splotched with cow pies. Someone had thoughtfully put two boards in the mud next to the water. I placed a knee on each board, gripped the front of the left board with my left hand, and searched for the cleanest place to dip my plastic Sawyer Squeeze container. Plant life swayed lazily beneath the cloudy water. Tiny minnows darted between the strands. I had to blow into the container to open it enough for the water to flow into it. I stretched out as far as I could and gently dipped the container into the water. It took its ever loving time filling up. I felt like I was in a one armed pushup position forever. I never did get it completely full. I pulled it out of the water, attached the filter, and squeezed the plastic container to get clean water to flow into one of my quart bottles. It filled the bottle about half way. I had to go through this same routine seven more times. Each time I would push the boards down into the mud a little deeper and get a little muddier. I looked and smelled rank. By the time I finished I had four quarts of clean, sparkling water. I worked hard to get that water. I was proud of those bottles. I even took a picture of them. Sadly, each time I took a sip the word "cow" came to mind. I was really regretting that generous offer from the rancher. Lesson learned: If you are ever offered water in the desert – Take It!

In a mile and a half I came to the end of the Bear Creek Gila Alternate Route. I would highly recommend it. I reconnected with the regular Continental Divide Trail. The road walk ended and the pathway headed up into the mountains. There was some strenuous hiking and my backpack weighed forty pounds. What a rookie! By 7:00 pm I was ready to call it a day. I fell asleep to the piercing call of elks.

The next morning started with a challenging climb. A heavy pack takes the joy out of hiking. My shoulders were aching and I was sweating heavily. By noon I was getting low on water. There was a spring a quarter of a mile off of the Trail. It wasn't listed as a WT source on Bear Creek's map and there wasn't a path to it but I needed water and decided to check it out. I never did find it but I did run into a dirt road that looked well used. It curved into the trees and I decided to follow it for ten minutes to see if I could find water. I hadn't seen any cattle but it looked like an area where cattle grazed. After ten minutes I was just about ready to turn back when I saw cattle drinking water from a tank. Yes! The earthen tank was full of brown disgusting looking water. It was surrounded by mud churned up by dozens of hoof prints and dotted with cow pies. There were even hoof prints in the water. When I saw the desperately needed water my eyes lit up with delight! As I approached the water the cattle scattered. I found a large flat stone and placed it in the mud beside the water. I kneeled on the stone and my weight pushed the stone down into the mud far enough that it started to collect on my legs. When I dipped the Sawyer Squeeze container into the water I could see brown silt flowing into the container and wondered if my filter would be able to handle it. When the container was full I attached the filter and squeezed amazingly clean clear water into my quart bottle. The Sawyer Squeeze filter was doing an outstanding job but the more I used it, the longer it took to squeeze clean water through it. It took about an hour to filter four quarts. As a precaution I added Aqua Mira Water Purification drops. It actually made the cow water taste better.

I could definitely have used some Kool Aid mix. I headed back to the Trail a happy hiker.

This was rugged hiking with long climbs and descents. I was in the 9,000 foot range passing through a boulder field and enjoying the beautiful views when I just about stepped on a dead elk. Talk about not paying attention! It looked like the elk had lost its balance on the rocks above, fallen onto boulders next to the Trail, and ended up partially on the Trail. Both of its front legs were broken. About a quarter mile later I started a descent into a jumbled area of rocks, boulders, downed trees, uneven clumps of grass, and dense foliage. I was really appreciating being on such a well-built trail. Just like that the Trail ended. I looked ahead and saw little flags on wires sticking out of the ground. The flags aligned with the proposed new pathway. They looked faded like they had been there a long time. I got out my GPS and started some heavy-duty bushwhacking. I loved that about the Continental Divide Trail. One minute I would be on a great trail and the next minute bushwhacking. It may eventually become a continuous well-worn path like the Appalachian Trail and the Pacific Crest Trail but being only about 76% complete I never knew what was going to happen next. I felt lucky to be hiking the CDT while it was still untamed. By the end of the day I was running low on water and exhausted. I wrote on my calendar: "May 21 - only 13.5 miles - worked hard for them - sometimes Trail just stopped - rocky - climbing over downed trees."

I was dragging the next morning as I started hiking. I began a steep descent and eventually made it to a gravel road. With the strenuous hiking and having to hydrate my beans and oatmeal, I was using a lot of water. I was down to a quart and planned only to take sips until I could find the next water source. Feeling deprived of water made me want it that much more. I didn't want a beer, or soft drink, or any other beverage. I wanted WATER! It was all I could think about. I could hear it trickling along a mountain stream. I could see perfectly choreographed jets of water shooting out of fountains and splashing into sparkling pools of clear blue water. I visualized an ice filled water pitcher with beads of moisture sliding down its sides. I would put that pitcher next to my cheek, shiver at its coolness, then take a big gulp and feel the cold wet water flowing down my parched throat. I took a moment from this reverie to take a selfie. It became the cover of this book. Notice my parched lips and grimy face. The CDT was beating me up and I was hurting. Badly!

The Continental Divide Trail will rub your nose in the dirt, make you say "Uncle!", then pick you up, gently dust you off, pat you on the back and say: "Look what I've got for you." Within minutes I saw a windmill with its blades flowing in the breeze. Beside the windmill was a big round tank filled with water. A long plastic pipe from the windmill was feeding water into the tank. The pipe reached far into the tank but someone had punctured the bottom of the pipe to create a hole close enough to the edge of the tank where I could fill my water bottles. It was a fairly calm day and I was at the mercy of the wind. Once the wind picked up the windmill creaked into motion - the wind wheel began to spin, the pump rod moved up and down, and within seconds water started flowing from the pipe. I put my water bottle under the pipe and watched it fill. It was half full when the wind stopped, which stopped the wind wheel, which stopped the pump rod, which stopped the flow of water. Aaaarrrgggg! At least there was enough water to take a drink. I was licking my lips in anticipation. That fresh out of the ground water tasted sooo good. Eventually, I drank two quarts just to quench my thirst. It took forty-five minutes to get my four water bottles filled.

3 PIE TOWN

Now that my belly was distended with water it was time to think PIES! Soon I would reach the Bear Creek Pie Town Alternate Route and a forty mile road walk to Pie Town, New Mexico. I couldn't wait! I had been thinking about pies since I first started planning a CDT thru-hike and looked up Pie Town on the internet. The 2010 census showed it had a population of 108. One of the two cafes in town was called the Pie-O-Neer. It had a menu with their pie list – Cherry-Cherry, Apple, Chocolate Cream (described as silky smooth, rich and dark), Luscious Lemon, Coca-Nana (Banana and Chocolate Cream combined), New Mexico Apple with Green Chile, Pumpkin with Whipped Cream, Chocolate Pecan, Coconut Cream (rated by Sunset Magazine as the "Best Pie In The West"), Green Chile Peach, Pecan, Strawberry-Rhubarb, Blueberry, Apple Cranberry Crumb, and Peach. By the time I started my hike I practically had that list memorized.

As I was hiking along on this twenty mile day I was trying to decide which pie I would start with. The chocolate cream pie sure sounded good, but there was the apple cranberry crumb to consider, I hadn't had a coconut cream pie in years and it was rated "Best Pie In The West" by Sunset Magazine. Decisions. Decisions. This was tough!

It was a cool, overcast day. I passed a decent water source but still had three quarts of water and a heavy pack and didn't follow my desert water plan of filling up at good sources. By 6:00 pm I started a long gradual climb. There was a listed water source a couple of miles past the summit. The climb became steeper and it was getting colder. The wind picked up and it started to sprinkle lightly. I put on my wind jacket. My hands were getting cold so I put on my gloves. The rain was beginning to soak my wind jacket and I added my rain jacket. The rain changed to light snow and I was getting cold. I reached the top of the mountain and the road headed down into the trees. Once off the top and out of the wind I started to warm up again. The snow ended and before long I reached the water source. It was a dirt tank that was completely dry. I didn't see any evidence of recent cattle activity. There was another tank in a mile but it was already dark so I decided to call it a night. I didn't sleep well. I only had a quart of water left. I had twenty-three miles to Pie Town and was worried the next water source would be dry. I was up and moving before dawn chanting my new mantra: "Please have water. Please have water." It didn't. Shit! Fortunately it was a cool, overcast day so I wouldn't need a lot of water and could pace myself until I could find another source. I was faced with a dilemma. The Pie-O-Neer Cafe closed at 4:00 pm and I had twenty-two miles to get there. I needed to get a move on but I was low on water and needed to pace myself. There was chocolate cream pie to be had. I'll bet you know which option I chose.

This was pleasant hiking through desert ranch land. I passed fenced in ranches with No Trespassing signs. There was very little traffic but everyone waved as they passed. A deeply tanned, weather worn, rancher stopped his pick-up truck to see what I was up to. We had an interesting conversation but my internal clock was screaming: "4:00 O'Clock! 4:00 O'Clock! Pie! Pie! Pie!" Wondering if he would take the hint I said: "I hear there is some excellent pie in Pie Town."

He laughed: "The best! I bet you want to have a piece. I won't keep you any longer. Have a great day!"

I had another dilemma. I was down to less than a quart of water. I needed that water desperately but I was also filthy. My legs were caked with road dust and dried mud mixed with cow manure. After filtering water at two cow tanks I had wiped my muddy hands on my shorts and shirt and they were covered with stains. I hadn't shaved since Silver City and my grimy face was covered with stubble. I smelled as bad as I looked. I knew it was a lost cause trying to clean up and would defy common sense using the water for anything but drinking, but I felt my funkiness was even below the standards of "hiker trash".

I seriously worried that when I reached the "Toaster House", Nita Larronde, the kind generous Trail Angel I had read so much about, whose house has been a haven for weary hikers since 1982, would take one look at me and say "keep going".

I made it to the Pie-O-Neer Café at 4:15 pm. I was late, but I wasn't above begging! I left my pack outside and headed to the door. There was a closed sign but the door wasn't locked so I went in. I was given a warm greeting by a tableful of hikers. Sitting at the table with them was Nita. She got up, came over to me, gave me a big smile, said Aloha, and wrapped me in a cheek to cheek bear hug. It just about floored me! I had heard many good things about her and I knew instantly she was the real deal.

Kathy Knapp, the very nice owner of the Pie-O-Neer told me the grill was being cleaned but asked if I wanted a piece of chocolate pecan pie.

"You bet!" I think the other hikers enjoyed watching me annihilate that pie. Kathy gave me another piece. I think she enjoyed watching me annihilate that excellent pie, too.

Soon we headed to the Toaster House. On the way, I stopped at the Post Office to pick up my resupply box. I still had more than enough food in my pack to make it to Grants, New Mexico so when I opened my resupply box I took out my new boots, Germ-X Hand Lotion, sunscreen and forwarded the food and everything else to Grants.

You can't miss the Toaster House. The entrance is a metal archway covered with old toasters. The exterior and interior of the house is an interesting collection of odds and ends accumulated over a period of many years. Nita raised her five children in this house. She doesn't live in the Toaster House any longer, she lives on a ranch outside of town, but she leaves the door unlocked and the house available for hikers, bicyclists, and motorcyclists passing through. When I arrived, there were six thru-hikers, a young couple bicycling cross country, and a motorcyclist in his sixties taking advantage of her hospitality.

Nita Larronde at the Toaster House

I wanted to get as much done as possible so I could take a true "zero" the next day. The washing machine was available and I washed my truly funky clothes. I headed to a nearby campground, took a long hot shower, shaved, and brushed my teeth. It felt good to be wearing clean clothes and feel clean. By the time I got back to the Toaster House, Walker was making dinner for everyone. It was fun listening to all the stories over dinner and later when everyone congregated outside on the big porch. It was interesting to hear stories from the perspective of bicyclists and a motorcyclist, too. It was a relaxed, congenial atmosphere and I stayed up well past hiker midnight.

I was out of bed by 6:00 the next morning and headed to the

kitchen to microwave some oatmeal. The kitchen table began to fill with hikers planning their day. Soon they were on their way but not before they washed the dishes, organized the bedrooms, and swept the house. This was a special place and we all knew it. There was a donation box in the kitchen and they made donations before they left. The house had been alive with energy then everyone was gone. It was so quiet – too quiet. I didn't have anything to do until lunch so I detailed the microwave until the interior was spotless and organized the pantry. After that I read some magazines. It felt good just to relax. It was a dark, blustery day and I was glad not to be hiking.

The Pie-O-Neer Café opened at 11:30 am and I was there by noon. This was Saturday, Memorial Day weekend, and it was packed. I joined Walker and Medic just as they were finishing their lunch and getting ready to head down the Trail. I couldn't keep from smiling. They started to leave then decided to get another piece of pie. This happened more than once. They stayed at the café almost as long as I did. This place was a hiker Vortex with a capital V. In addition to the pies, the menu consisted of two choices – green chili stew or a quiche. I chose the green chili stew. As I was waiting for my food I was caught up in the energy of the place. It was bustling. Kathy had her oven mitt on and was taking freshly baked pies out of the big oven. As soon as pies came out, pies went in to replace them. It was non-stop the whole time I was there. Customers ordered whole pies to go plus she was meeting the pie needs of a full restaurant. The place smelled of freshly baked pies. The green chili stew arrived along with a big warm tortilla. It was the best green chili stew I have ever tasted! Period! They didn't skimp on the portions either.

Now was the moment I had been waiting for. I ordered the chocolate cream pie. I ate it slowly, enjoying the silky smooth rich dark chocolate. Oh my Gosh! I didn't think it was possible, but it happened. My mother was a champion when it came to baking pies. She used Crisco to make a light, flaky crust that was unmatched. Her chocolate pie was my favorite. I always asked for it when I was a child and when I would visit as an adult. Over the years I had eaten hundreds of pieces of chocolate pie in restaurants and homes throughout the country. Often they were good, sometimes very good, occasionally they were excellent, but they never matched the standard set by my mother. The chocolate cream pie at the Pie-O-Neer Café reminded me of my mother's chocolate pie. It was perfect! There was a whole enticing menu of pies to choose from but after I finished the first piece I had to have another piece of chocolate cream pie. It was almost nostalgic as I savored every bite.

I headed back to the Toaster House a satisfied, genuinely happy hiker. I was surprised to see that I had the place to myself. I kept expecting other hikers to show up but they never did. This was a comfortable house. The living room had big comfortable chairs, a large comfortable sofa, and tables covered with magazines of varying ages. A book shelf filled with books covered one of the walls. There were nick knacks and do dads and the accumulation of years of living. I checked out the bedrooms to find a place to sleep. Her children had been given free rein to give their bedrooms their own personal touch. The room I chose had a basketball hoop over the door, bunk beds, and a big comfortable chair for reading. The bedroom next door was dark blue and filled with stars painted on the walls and ceiling. I never did check to see if they glowed in the night. There was an upstairs bedroom that was a newer addition to the house with bunk beds and enough room to sleep six people. The bathroom had a washer and dryer. The kitchen had a microwave and an old wood burning oven. The kitchen table was where everyone congregated. Next to the table was an impressive hiker box. It included a plastic bag with at least thirty AA batteries. A full pantry had all kinds of food left by hikers. There was a large porch with comfortable chairs. The wall of the house next to the porch had hooks with used hiker shoes and boots attached. Some of them were completely destroyed while others looked like they might have more miles left in them. I hung my Keens on the wall. They had 800 miles on them and had served me well. On the back porch was a refrigerator with frozen pizza, donuts, and other food left by previous hikers. This was a house totally geared to hiker's needs.

In the evening I was sitting on the sofa reading a Smithsonian Magazine when Nita stopped by for a visit. She grew up in Hawaii and greeted me with an Aloha. It was a pleasure talking with her. She told me that after she moved in she started seeing people with backpacks walking by her house. Finally she stopped a young couple and asked them what they were doing. They told her they were hiking the Continental Divide Trail and the Trail was the road that passed by her house. This made her curious so she invited them in to learn more about this Continental Divide Trail and the people who hiked it. The rest is history. The number of people that have stayed at the Toaster House over the years is well into the thousands. She told me as her children were growing up it broadened their horizons to meet people from all over the United States and the world. Before she left I took her picture standing next to all the toasters. Here is a woman who is generous, has the respect and admiration of the hiking community, and enjoys being part of it. What a genuinely good lady.

By the time I was ready for bed it was windy and cold and I covered myself with two blankets. A big thunderstorm came through at 9:00 pm and I snuggled deeper under the blankets just pleased as punch to be right where I was.

Before leaving the next morning I put $40 into the donation box and added my compliments to Nita's hiker logbook. Meeting Nita and staying at the Toaster House was another highlight of my hike. Such good vibrations! The stormy weather passed through in the night and I started the day under blue skies. A couple of miles out of town I picked up Bear Creek's Cebolla Wilderness Alternate Route and followed it for fifty miles. There was very little traffic on this well maintained dirt road, it was a cool pleasant day, and I hiked twenty-eight miles. The road headed through parched ranch land and past foul looking cow tanks. I passed ranches surrounded by barbed wire and signs with forbidding warnings: No Trespassing Under ANY Circumstances   No Trespassing For ANY Reason. Wow! No problem. Sometimes there were archways over the gates that had metal silhouettes with the name of the ranch and a cowboy on horseback lassoing a cow, or deer grazing, or Dad, Mom, and the three kids wearing Stetsons.

Eventually I came to a ranch house with a wide open gate, an American flag flapping in the breeze, and a sign that said "Welcome". It was like a breath of fresh air. The house belonged to John and Anzie Thomas, a kind couple in their eighties who welcomed hikers to fill up their water bottles and visit. I still had plenty of water and it didn't look like anyone was home, so I continued on. I heard many good things about the Thomas's. What a great way for an older couple in an isolated area to stay connected.

This was easy hiking on a straight road and I was making better miles than expected. I knew eventually I had to make a sharp turn to the east to connect with Armijo Canyon. By the time I checked my GPS I was a quarter mile past the turn off. It was 8:00 pm and I decided to call it a night. I didn't want to be noticed by anyone driving by so I camped one hundred yards from the road. It turned out to be one of my favorite camping spots. As I put up my tent I watched the whole western sky turn a beautiful shade of red. Ten cows were quietly grazing nearby. It was a still night and I could hear them pulling up grass and chewing. I picked up on their tranquility. I tried to stay awake to enjoy it but was asleep within minutes of getting into my sleeping bag. This was a vast area. The cattle could have grazed anywhere. A couple of times in the night I woke up and they were still peacefully grazing only a hundred feet away. There was an occasional low "mooo".

The next morning, I said goodbye to my bovine friends, headed back to the turnoff and followed a dirt road until it entered the forest at Armijo Canyon. A couple of miles into this beautiful canyon I stopped at a long abandoned homestead. The house looked quite old. It was on a knoll with a picturesque view. It would be considered small by today's standards but in its time it was a house to be proud of. There was even a wide kitchen window next to the sink. I could almost see Mrs. Armijo glancing out of that window as she went about her kitchen chores. I went inside. The thick walls had been gouged out in places and there was extensive damage to the roof. Graffiti covered the interior walls, some of it dating back to the 1970's. It was sad to see this once loved home in such a state of deterioration.

The Trail headed steeply out of the canyon on an old faded road and connected with Sand Canyon in a couple of miles. I hiked through this rugged canyon admiring its red tinged sandstone walls. Where Sand Canyon connected with Cebolla Canyon there was a windmill I had listed as "good water" on my map. It was a little bit off trail but an excellent source. I filled my five bottles then sat down next to the windmill and had some lunch. The windmill creaked and groaned as it filled a big water tank for the cattle. Someday I want to camp near a windmill and be lulled to sleep by that lonely, mournful sound.

I hiked through a sandy area for three more miles before reaching a paved two lane highway. My goal was to follow the highway for twelve miles and stop for the night at the Zuni-Acoma Trailhead. I walked on the side of the road facing traffic. Cars would come by about every five minutes. Once they were within a hundred feet I would get off of the pavement and walk in the dirt. It was a warm day, heat radiated off of the pavement, and I was glad to have five quarts of water. After about a mile, John and Anzie Thomas, who were on their way to Grants, pulled their truck to the side of the road and asked if I needed water. Such nice people. They were looking out for their hikers. I still had five quarts so I declined. The highway headed in a straight line for three miles before it swung to the left. Once I reached the turnoff I could see my new route for miles in the distance as it went up the side of a mountain. It was a groan worthy moment. The scenery was impressive, though. On my right, colorful sandstone walls towered above the road. On my left was a vast forbidding area of lava called the Malpais.

Where the road began to climb I had a notation on my map: "Possible drug area. Don't camp." Sure enough, it was. A pickup truck stopped beside me. The young couple didn't even pull to the side of the road. Both of them looked at me but didn't attempt to solicit. I just glanced at them as I passed by and they moved on. A hundred yards further, a lady in a SUV stopped right on the road. She waited for me to make the first move. When she saw I wasn't interested she took off. I'm glad I had been warned; otherwise it would have been confusing.

After a twenty-five mile day I made it to the Zuni-Acoma Trailhead by 7:00 pm and found a good camping spot next to small pinion trees. Once I set up my tent I sat down on the soft sandy dirt to eat my dinner. A little beetle headed out from a clump of grass took one look at me and shot away as fast as it could go. I thought it would eventually slow down but, if anything, it picked up speed and stayed totally animated for twenty feet until it turned a corner and was out of sight. I often encountered these beetles while hiking. One would be walking on the Trail, see me, and immediately stick its head in the dirt and its butt straight up in the air. "I'm hiding. You can't see me." It was always good for a smile.

4 GRANTS, NEW MEXICO

Hugo and Carole Mumm, a retired couple living in Grants, are wonderful Trail Angels. They had a water cache for hikers at the Zuni-Acoma Trailhead. There were twenty-two more miles to Grants and the water was greatly appreciated. I headed out the next morning at 7:00 am. I was finally down to less than a pound of the twenty-two pounds of food I started with at Doc Campbell's Store. I had travelled 190 miles on that resupply. My pack weighed less than twenty pounds and I was a happy hiker! The miles went by fast. Before long I crossed the bridge over Interstate 40 and could see Grants far in the distance. It was hard to contain my eagerness. Once I had Grants in sight it felt like it took forever to get there - so close and yet so far. I made it by 2:00 pm and headed to the Motel 6. Just before the motel was a Subway restaurant. I had hiked 28, 25, and 22 miles in the last three days and I was hungry! The motel could wait. Priorities... After a filling Subway salad, foot long chicken teriyaki sub crammed with vegetables, and three chocolate chip cookies, I headed to the Motel 6. It had a tall sign with a $39 rate to attract Interstate 40 traffic. As I was checking in, the desk clerk asked for my identification. When this honest lady calculated my rate, she included a senior discount without my even asking. The total amount I paid for a night's stay was $40.62. The discount was like getting a Subway foot long for free. She didn't have to do that. I wouldn't have noticed. I love it when these little unexpected jewels show up.

It felt good to take a shower then relax on a clean, soft bed. I was asleep by 8:00 pm and slept ten solid hours. The next morning I lounged around watching TV until the 11:00 am check out time. I was still in no hurry. I didn't want to get to the South San Juan Mountains too early and have to deal with a lot of snow. For much of my hike I had experienced unseasonably cool weather for New Mexico. Many days I would wear my wind shirt until noon. It hadn't rained much but often there were dark clouds overhead. This had me worried. The snow pack in the Colorado mountains had been average when I left on my hike. Were the mountains getting additional snow from all the weather systems passing through? Having spent very little time around snow, I knew I needed to take the snow levels seriously. I called my brother and asked him to send an ice axe to Chama, New Mexico. The ice axe I planned to use was out of stock so he contacted the Hiking Forum of Trail Journals (www.trailjournals.com) to get suggestions on the best ice axe to use. Jerry Brown, whose Bear Creek Maps and GPS waypoints were extremely accurate and kept me oriented on my hike, gave his recommendation. My brother took it and by the time I reached Chama a new ice axe was waiting for me. Thanks Doug and Bearcreek.

I headed to the Post Office to pick up my resupply box. The Trail followed Route 66 through the heart of town. After the uranium mines shut down, Grants never totally recovered. I passed boarded up shops, boarded up motels, and motels with prices in the low $30 range that looked to be struggling. My resupply box had food for the next 107 mile leg to Cuba, New Mexico. I planned on six days to get there. When I made up my food boxes before the hike, for some reason that is beyond me, I figured on three pounds a day. Since Doc Campbell's, I had been eating two and a half pounds a day just to lower the total food weight. It was more than I would normally need this early in a hike but my body was accepting it and it was giving me a lot of energy. I decided to lower the daily food weight to two pounds and see how my body handled it. I forwarded the rest of the food to Cuba. Looking on the bright side of my miscalculations – I spent very little money on groceries in New Mexico and spent the money saved enjoying enormous amounts of food in cafes and restaurants.

It was 2:00 pm by the time I headed out of town. There was a four mile road walk then the CDT followed a steep winding pathway to the top of Horace Mesa. I stayed on the mesa top the rest of the day. Looking back I could see Grants far in the distance. Dark clouds behind me were slowly catching up and there was an occasional rumble of thunder. I was constantly looking over my shoulder expecting the rain to hit at any minute. I finally bailed. It was only 6:00 pm but what the heck! I found a great spot to camp in a thick grove of oak trees. The heavy rain never materialized. Rain lightly pattered on my tent and a cool breeze gently rustled the leaves. I was sound asleep by 8:00 pm and slept until 6:00 the next morning. Two days in a row with ten hours of solid sleep. My body must have needed it because I awoke refreshed and ready to tackle the day.

I spent most of the day climbing and descending through

pine forests in the 8,000' to 9,500' range near the base of Mt. Taylor. I considered it, but decided not to take the alternate route to the top. Living in New Mexico, I had already been to the top on earlier hikes. Rain threatened for most of the day and I stopped after only sixteen miles. I found a place to camp in a narrow canyon in a meadow surrounded by tall ponderosa pines. A thunderstorm was heading my way and I managed set up my tent and get in right as the rain hit. Deep angry thunder reverberated off of the narrow canyon walls and pounding wind and rain buffeted my sturdy tent. I was grateful not to be on top of Mt. Taylor.

After the cleansing rain, the pine forest smelled wonderful as I started my hike the next morning. Soon I was out of the forest. The rest of the day was spent hiking through wide open range land. I followed Argentina's shoe prints for miles. I had been seeing his shoe prints off and on since I met him on day four of my journey. Now it was day twenty-seven and I had hiked 484 miles. Argentina was still the only thru-hiker I had seen on the Trail. Sometimes it would be days between Argentina shoe print sightings but when those size 13 Cascadia 7's did show up it gave me a weird pleasure. I actually started talking to them: "Argentina! Haven't seen you in a while." I know it sounds crazy, but it gave me a feeling of companionship. It was kind of like Tom Hanks in "Cast Away" talking to his volleyball companion "Wilson".

Twenty-two miles into the day I made it to Los Indios Spring. It was a half mile off trail and down in a canyon but the piped water was bountiful, cold, pure, and tasted wonderful. Tall aspen trees were providing cool shade so I stopped for dinner. Before leaving, I drank another quart of the delicious water then hiked two more miles before putting my tent under a massive oak tree.

The climb to start the morning was tough but when I reached the ridge the views were outstanding. I hiked along the top of a mesa for the next seven miles. Far to the north I could see Cabezon Peak, an isolated volcanic plug rising over 1000' above the surrounding canyons, arroyos, and mesas. Without looking at my map I had a feeling I would soon be visiting those canyons and sure enough I hiked the next eight miles through canyon after canyon. I loved it! This was New Mexico at its high desert best with its arroyos, washes, hoodoos, ravines, gorges, gulches, gullies, buttes, cactus, pinion, juniper, creosote, sage, chamisa, shale, small rocks, big rocks, boulders and gorgeous sandstone walls. I managed to get lost in a wide sandy arroyo and was pissed when I had to backtrack through the thick sand.

The temperature was 90 degrees in this parched unforgiving desert and places to find shade were few and far between. I was working hard for the miles and my body was demanding water. Eventually the Trail climbed out of the canyons and into pasture land. I had been limiting my water intake and was really looking forward to completely quenching my thirst at the next well.

The next well was dry. Damn! There was a dead cow a few feet away. Its teeth were clinched in an eerie grin and the roasting sun had turned it into little more than bleached bones and dehydrated hide. I looked at my map. The next water was a private well eight miles away. I had marked on my map – "piped water". I was sure this one would have water. As I headed out my dejected body language said it all.

The lack of water was not only affecting my mood, it was affecting my stamina. I was dragging. I finally reached the turn-off to the well. There was even a sign that pointed the way. Great! Not so great. It was dry as a bone! I was down to less than a quart and the next water was seven miles further. There was nothing to do but trudge on. I reached a paved road and a couple of cars passed by. By now it was dark. If the next source didn't have water, I could hitch to the nearest town, but I would have to wait until morning and my body desperately needed water. I remembered my Pacific Crest Trail thru-hike where I ran low on water and started pissing blood. The next source HAD to have water. I was now down to four ounces. The two mile trek to the water was difficult. I was trying hard to be optimistic but after two dry wells in a row I was mentally preparing for another disappointment. It was 9:30 pm by the time I arrived. I had never felt a thirst like the one I was feeling. I headed to a two foot wide cylinder buried in the ground and looked down a five foot shaft. At the bottom was an inch of water. Unless I went in head first - which was crazy – the cylinder was too narrow to get to the water. I couldn't just give up. There was water at the bottom of that shaft and I had to find a way to get it. I grabbed a water bottle, leaned into the cylinder, and put my arm down as far as I could reach. I was about a foot short. I tried again, leaned down as far as I dared, felt my balance wobble, and just about fell head first into the cylinder. I needed that water desperately! It was inches from my grasp - Tantalizing me! Taunting me! My mind reluctantly came to the realization that I couldn't reach it. "Damn!"

My throat was so dry the word came out as a hoarse whisper. This was serious. I needed to stay calm and focused and figure a way out of this mess. I had "water tank" listed on my map and started looking for the tank. Twenty feet from the cylinder the light from my headlamp spotted a gallon container of water. What a Treasure! I put that container to my lips and started drinking. The water tasted glorious! My mind was telling me to stop and conserve it, but my emotions were telling me I needed water NOW! I kept chugging non-stop until half of the container was gone. My thirst was slaked but I let my emotions cloud my judgement. I was down to just two quarts of water. What if the next water source was dry? What about the hikers behind me? I would be taking all the water and leaving them high and dry. I always thought I would share in times of need but I needed that water and I took it. I felt guilty. I tried to justify it. It was muddy around the cylinder. There were times when it was so full it overflowed. Maybe the next people through would find water. (It turned out Medic and Walker did find water the next day.) I should have been elated but I felt depressed and guilt-ridden. It was late so I didn't bother with dinner. I put my tent in a lumpy field next to a cow path. Cows came by in the night, I could feel the lumpy grass through my air mattress, my stomach was growling, and I didn't get much sleep. I had a terrible dream. I know it was caused by the guilt of not sharing.

Around 5:00 in the morning I heard a bull in a nearby canyon. He was slowly moving in my direction and bellowing so I quickly packed up and headed on my way. After three miles I started a steep climb past Deadman Peak and onto a mesa. Once on top, I found a pleasantly cool spot in a morning shadow to take a break. As I was enjoying my oatmeal with raisins I was within feet of the mesa rim looking down on canyons and arroyos being hit by the first rays of sunlight. Far on the horizon I could see the outline of Cabezon Peak. It brought back pleasant memories. Cabezon Peak had been my landmark on flights between Farmington and Albuquerque, New Mexico.

In the early 80's I was a pilot for a commuter airline based in Farmington, New Mexico. One of my jobs was to fly the afternoon route from Farmington to Albuquerque and back. Five days a week I would fly right over where I was now having breakfast and see the pinion covered mesa, colorful eroded sandstone canyons, and vast range land slashed by steep walled arroyos. I saw this beautiful desert covered in winter snow, green from monsoon rains, and parched from summer heat. I remember thinking: "Someday I would love to explore this area." Now I was actually doing it! What was even better – this gorgeous land was even more impressive from the ground than it was from the air.

The Trail followed the mesa wall for miles. At times I was next to the edge looking straight down. It was interesting seeing how nature had carved the beautiful sandstone canyons. Seventeen miles into the day's hike I came to the first potential water source. I had written on my map: "Hole in sandstone that might hold water." At the base of a sandstone cliff was a beautiful little five foot long, three foot wide basin that caught rainwater rolling down the side of the cliff. It looked to be about three feet deep and three-quarters full. There were bugs in it and a little scum on the surface but otherwise it looked pretty good. This was a water source for animals in this dry country and probably had been for tens of thousands of years. I only filtered a quart and drank it, then filtered another quart to take with me. That gave me enough water to make it the seventeen miles to Cuba, New Mexico. The water was cool and tasted good. It was a shady area and I took a food break by the little waterhole. I was packing up when around the corner came a young, fit, extremely energetic hiker. It startled me. The last people I had seen hiking on the Trail had been the two teenaged girls as I was descending to the Gila River. That had been on the 15th of May. It was now June 1st. I hiked with Lorax for about ten minutes. He was talkative, considerate, and patient, but he had a goal of reaching Cuba, New Mexico and having dinner at El Bruno's Mexican Restaurant with his ex-girlfriend's father and I could see he was about ready to explode with barely contained energy. I wished him luck and he shot away. We were on a long steep climb and I could see him getting farther and farther ahead. It was 3:00 pm when I met him and seventeen miles to Cuba. If he made it to dinner with his ex-girlfriend's father by 7:00 pm he would have to average over four miles per hour. This was hard hiking. I didn't see how he could possibly make it in time. I learned later that he made it. Sigh.....To be twenty-three again.

I made my way to Jones Canyon and started looking for Jones Spring. I had a notation on my map: "Good Water". I was grumbling to myself: "Yea. Right....Probably NO water!" The spring was beside an overhanging cliff. The area was filled with shady trees and lush vegetation. The water was piped into a metal trough. I looked into the trough and there were tiny organisms squiggling around. A sign said to filter the water and I did. I filled all four of my quart bottles and drank an extra quart before I left. It felt good to drink until I was completely full. Leaving Jones Canyon I hiked a couple of miles through a valley. Some highly creative person had punched holes into tin to make CDT signs. I passed a number of them in this area. Leaving the valley I made a very challenging climb to the top of Mesa Portales. This one really had my attention. There were a couple of times I put my hiking stick into my backpack and used my hands to work my way up. For the rest of the day I hiked along the rim of the mesa enjoying great views. I hiked twenty-two miles and worked for them. The temperature had been in the low nineties and it immediately began to cool after the sun set. I found a spot for my tent within feet of the edge of Mesa Portales with views to a far horizon. There wasn't a cloud in the sky or a hint of breeze. It looked like a perfect night to use just the netting on my tent. It was the best night of my hike. By the time I finished dinner it was dark and I got into my sleeping bag. My weary body was completely relaxed after a long day of hiking and I could feel myself falling asleep. Soon I was snoring peacefully. I woke up once in the night and opened my eyes to an absolutely dazzling display of stars. Unless you have experienced it, it is hard to imagine how bright the night sky can be without competition from city lights. I just lay there gazing at the stars; totally mesmerized. I was exactly where I wanted to be, doing exactly what I wanted to be doing. What a great way to spend my retirement!

5 CUBA, NEW MEXICO

I awoke the next morning refreshed and eager to tackle the nine miles to Cuba. I had a beef and bean burrito with green chili on my mind and was hiking at over four miles an hour. In four miles I reached the highway, then hiked along the shoulder for five miles as cars and trucks whizzed by. Once I reached town I registered at the motel, headed to my room, and took a long cleansing shower. I had the rest of the day to casually take care of town chores. I headed to the Post Office to pick up the resupply box I had forwarded from Grants and the resupply box sent from home. The resupply box from Grants had enough food to get to my next stop at Ghost Ranch. I forwarded the resupply box from home to Ghost Ranch. I also picked up a letter from my sister, Johanna. Before I start a hike Johanna always asks for a list of the towns where I am going to stop. When we talk on the phone she lets me know if I have a letter at the next town. I look forward to those letters. They keep me updated on what's happening with her family, have questions about my hike, and she always includes a $20 bill. My eyes light up when I see that $20 bill. To me it's a $20 pig out for free! With that in mind I headed to the nearest restaurant and got my $20's worth. By the end of the day I had hit two Mexican restaurants, a Subway, and stopped at the grocery store for a fruit platter - an excellent town day!

The next morning I headed to the Cuban Café for breakfast. My next door neighbor, Sheryl Roos, told me she and her husband, Joe, had stopped there many times and the food was ample and good. She wasn't kidding. I sat down at a table and looked at the menu. The breakfast burrito caught my eye. It was the most expensive item on the menu. I ordered it. The waitress glanced at my skinny little body and looked skeptical. "This is really big...." She glanced at me again. I felt like I was being appraised and coming up short. "Bring it on!" I said with bravado. She shrugged and filled my coffee cup. I felt kind of insulted. I was going to show her what a hiker appetite was all about. When I finished the breakfast burrito I was going to casually order a short stack of pancakes just to watch her reaction. When the breakfast burrito arrived it was the biggest burrito I had seen in my life! It completely filled an extra-large plate. I said under my breath: "Holy Shit!" The waitress looked at me like: "I warned you..." I plowed right in. Soon I was half-way through; then three-quarters of the way through. I noticed I was getting more coffee refills. I had the waitress's attention and possibly grudging admiration? By now I was stuffed but not about to give up. The last few bites were a struggle but when I finished, my plate didn't have a crumb on it. The waitress came over. "More coffee?" She looked me in the eye, gave me a little nod, and big smile.

The CDT followed the highway through Cuba. It was like old home week passing all the familiar places on my way out of town. I had driven through Cuba on my way to hike and camp in the San Pedro Mountains since the late 70's and was really looking forward to this section. The San Pedro Parks Wilderness is just about my favorite spot on earth. It is less than two hours from my home and many times over the years I have spent a weekend, week, two weeks, and even a month enjoying its beauty. It is not difficult hiking. You gradually head up through pines, aspen, and spruce to a long, wide plateau in the ten thousand foot range. You cross clear mountain streams and hike along wide grassy meadows called parks. A lot of the time these green meadows are still wet with snow melt and you do a lot of sloshing and hopping from one clump of grass to the next. Separating the meadows are thick stands of tall spruce. In late fall, coated with snow, they are magnificent! Often you see elk, sometimes large herds of elk, wild turkeys, bears, and coyotes.

In 2011 I spent a month camping in the San Pedro Mountains. On one of my daily hikes, high in the mountains, I stopped next to a long abandoned turquoise mine. To the southwest was a stunning view of canyon land all the way to Mt. Taylor and beyond. It looked like an incredibly far distance to travel on foot but it also looked challenging. At that moment I knew I had to hike the Continental Divide Trail. Now on this lovely day I was hiking the Continental Divide Trail and heading to the San Pedro Parks Wilderness. It didn't get much better than that.

Leaving Cuba, I followed Los Pinos Road for miles until it became Los Pinos Trail and headed into the forest. Once I was under the canopy of trees I heard raindrops. Impossible. It was a clear sunny day. I looked up and hundreds of tiny fuzzy caterpillars were dropping from the trees. The ground was covered with them. One hit my neck and started to slide down my back. I automatically slapped it and left a gooey mess on my neck and hand. Yuck! I was surprised there were so few birds taking advantage of this bounty. I hiked beside the Rio Puerco and crossed the Rio de las Vacas. After 525 miles of dry desert it was a joy seeing sparkling mountain streams. The Trail headed into aspen groves. I know I shouldn't, and wouldn't consider contributing, but I have always found graffiti on aspen trees entertaining. I look for the most ancient graffiti and try to imagine the person (long since dead) standing right where I'm standing, carving his name and the date into the tree. The oldest carving I found in the San Pedro's was dated 1898, written in Spanish in an elegant scroll, and still perfectly clear. It looked like a deed with numbers and a signature at the bottom.

After some enjoyable graffiti searching, I came out of the forest and caught my first glimpse of the San Pedro Parks. In the distance were green healthy meadows separated by tall spruce trees. I was back in my old stomping grounds. I stopped for a break to enjoy the moment. Trail Dog and CDT Marmot caught up to me. We chatted for a while then they headed on. It was a pleasure meeting thru-hikers in my age range. I watched as they got smaller and smaller before they entered one of the meadows and were out of sight.

After watching Trail Dog and CDT Marmot, I knew where the Trail headed. Soon I entered the meadow where I saw them disappear. It was boggy and I was doing a lot of maneuvering to keep my feet dry. I remembered my Cocker Spaniel, Wingo, trying to negotiate one of those soggy meadows. I could see him bounding from one clump of grass to the next and eventually falling into the water. He then started bounding through the water trying to catch up to me. When he caught up, I stopped to congratulate him. "Good dog, Wingo!" He proceeded to shake his thick Cocker Spaniel coat and totally soak me. He looked up at me like: "Isn't this fun?"………not so much………I spent the next hours seeing familiar sites – places where I had camped and hiked twenty, even thirty years earlier. It brought back good memories. I caught up to Trail Dog and CDT Marmot in the afternoon and we stayed together the rest of the day. We chatted as we hiked. They invited me to camp with them in a beautiful area high in the San Pedro Peaks Wilderness.

Our elevation when we started the next morning was over 10,000 feet and the views were superb. Eventually the Trail headed down the mountain. I caught up to Trail Dog and CDT Marmot taking a break by a little spring and joined them. Delicious spring water flowed right out of the mountain.

In the afternoon I was hiking through thick forest and came to a dirt road. I passed a corral and continued on the road for three quarters of a mile before it connected with a well-travelled pathway. I followed the pathway for a quarter of a mile. My GPS said the next waypoint was slightly to the east but I figured there would be a correction so I continued on. The pathway began to fade. I knew I was off course but kept waiting for the correction. Soon I was bushwhacking through dense thorny undergrowth, hopping over downed trees, and my legs were covered with bloody scratches. I looked to the east. Not good. To get back on course I would have to cross a dry streambed and climb an extremely steep 300 foot embankment. I crossed the streambed and stared up at the daunting climb ahead. The prudent course of action would be to backtrack to the road and get re-oriented but that would be a pain in the butt. Naw! I can do this. As I started the climb my boots were sliding on the loose soil and I was using my hands to maneuver up the hill. Downed trees blocked the way and I would scramble over them or work my way around them. I needed to be totally focused so the weight of my backpack didn't cause me to topple backwards. This was tough hiking! I stopped for a break. Sweat was flowing down my forehead and I could feel the burn in my legs. My lungs were burning, too. Since I was hiking alone I didn't have the luxury of an icy glare and the question: "Whose bright idea was this, anyway?" After the break I continued to climb. My legs were getting wobbly. Eventually I could see the outline of a dirt road and my GPS showed the waypoint to be right on the road. Once I was on the road and oriented I had a chance to assess the situation. Damn! That was fun!

Within a mile I came to a trailhead surrounded by tall pines and called it a day. I set my tent on a matting of pine needles and made some dinner. I was waiting for Trail Dog and CDT Marmot to show up but by 8:00 pm they still hadn't arrived so I figured they probably found another place to camp. A little bird was my only companion. Its crystal clear song filled the air. At 8:30 pm I heard sounds outside of my tent. It was Trail Dog and CDT Marmot! Their adrenaline was still pumping. They started telling me of an adventure they had just been through. I realized they made the same turn at the well-travelled pathway, the same decision to keep moving forward, and the same miserable climb to get back on course – a shared misadventure. We had a good laugh. We learned later we were not the only ones to be confused by that well-travelled pathway.

6 GHOST RANCH

Our goal the next day was to hike eighteen miles to Ghost Ranch and make it there in time for dinner. We decided to take the following day off to rest and recharge. The Gila River, Pie Town, San Pedro Parks Wilderness, and Ghost Ranch were the highlights I most wanted to experience in New Mexico. My sister, Johanna, and I are big Georgia O'Keeffe fans. A few years ago we went to the Georgia O'Keeffe Art Museum in Santa Fe, took a tour of her home in Abiquiu, New Mexico, and visited Ghost Ranch where she also had a home. The physical beauty of Ghost Ranch was magnificent. Its green fields and large shady trees seemed to blend with the gorgeous multi-colored canyons and mountains. After the first visit I knew I wanted to come back someday.

As we started our hike to Ghost Ranch I had a spring in my step. We headed down a steep winding pathway until we reached Ojillos Canyon; then followed the canyon for five miles to the Rio Chama. We passed stunning mountains with red, orange, brown, and yellow sandstone walls. Trail Dog and CDT Marmot were far ahead and I could see their hats and packs weaving through the dense sage. We finally made it to the Rio Chama, crossed Skull Bridge, and followed the Bear Creek alternate trail for the next eleven miles to Ghost Ranch. The landscape that Ghost Ranch is known for started to come into view. I saw a mountain with a flat narrow mesa top that looked familiar - Cerro Pedernal! It was like I was looking at a Georgia O'Keeffe painting! Soon I could see the tree filled outline of Ghost Ranch nestled beside red tinged canyons. From the abandoned visitor's center there was a two mile trail to Ghost Ranch with little signs describing the flora and fauna. I followed it until it started to meander then made a bee line up and down hills straight to the ranch.

Ghost Ranch is hiker friendly. The staff goes out of their way to be helpful and make you feel welcome. There is simple lodging with meals included, a library open 24 hours a day, free use of the computer, and free Wi-Fi. I signed in at the registration office and was given directions to the campground. Camping is free to hikers the first day. I found a nice spot to put my tent and headed over to the campground's shower and laundry. I wanted to get as much done as possible so I could focus on dinner. If you are a thru-hiker, by the time you reach Ghost Ranch your hiker appetite is raging. Imagine eating three all-you-can-eat meals a day of extremely good, healthy food. A chef even supervises the preparation of the meals. Breakfast is $7, lunch $10, dinner $12, and you get more than your money's worth.

Dinner was in a large dining hall, served cafeteria style, and all that I hoped for. There was a big salad bar that I took advantage of, too. Heading back to my tent I was feeling full and happy and drowsy. I was asleep before it was even dark and slept ten solid hours.

The next morning I met Trail Dog and CDT Marmot for

breakfast. The food was so freaking good! I loaded up with fresh fruit. During a thru-hike I can put away a lot of food. I noticed I was just holding my own with Trail Dog and CDT Marmot. It felt good to be enjoying healthy foods that were missing from my diet while hiking.

Ghost Ranch is an education and retreat center operated by the Presbyterian Church that offers classes in subjects like silversmithing, pottery making, weaving, fused glass landscapes, pastel painting, holistic medicine, yoga, snowshoeing, rock climbing, birdwatching, spirituality, and much more. It caters to all age groups. The atmosphere is of people coming together to learn and have an enjoyable experience. It is a positive and relaxing atmosphere.

After breakfast, the day went by a lot faster than I anticipated. I headed to the registration office to pick up my resupply box and was pointed to a little room crammed full of hiker boxes. Everything is on the honor system at Ghost Ranch. I sorted through the boxes until I found mine and walked back to my tent to organize my backpack. When I finished it was time to meet Trail Dog and CDT Marmot for lunch. Even after the huge breakfast I was more than ready for lunch. I focused on quantity, of course, but this time I tweaked it and zeroed in on decadence. There were big, thick chocolate brownies mixed with just a hint of peanut butter to die for. I had three of them. There wasn't much conversation as we plowed into the food but our happy faces said it all.

After lunch we went to the visitor's center to look at maps and plan our route to Chama, New Mexico. Since there was snow along the route we decided to road walk from Ghost Ranch to Chama. I normally hike alone but was glad to be hiking with Ted and Peggy. I enjoyed their company. We had a lot to talk about and our conversations were relaxed and effortless. Since we weren't around other hikers we started using our given names. I spent some time on the computer and stayed in the air conditioned visitor's center until it was time to meet them for dinner. Dinner was excellent and I ate until I was stuffed. I could almost feel my body rebuilding muscle and storing glycogen for the hike ahead. After dinner we sat in the shade of massive cottonwoods, relaxed, and talked until dark.

One more amazing breakfast and we were ready to hit the road. My stay at Ghost Ranch left me rested, recharged, and ready to go. I felt genuinely welcome at Ghost Ranch and look forward to my next visit.

The next leg of our journey was a forty-four mile road walk to Chama. I wasn't thrilled at the prospect of a road walk but it turned out to be quite scenic. We walked facing traffic on the narrow apron of Highway 84. My little road walk guide showed that we would be reaching a convenience store in the afternoon and I was looking forward to an iced cold coke. Clouds began building early in the day and by 4:00 pm nasty dark clouds were closing in. Areas on either side of us were getting pounded by rain but by some miracle it hadn't reached us yet. We topped a hill and could see the convenience store in the distance. It was a race to see if we could make it there in time. We couldn't hike any faster without jogging and made it in the nick of time. The minute I was inside and closed the door, it was so quiet and serene. I realized how much I had been fighting the wind. The store had a small bar and we headed to it. The whole interior of the bar, even the ceiling, was decorated with signed one dollar bills. Peggy microwaved a pizza and we had pizza and coke while we waited out the rain. It gave me great pleasure watching the wind swept rain battering the bar's windows.

The weather was improving when we started hiking an hour later. By 7:00 pm we began looking for a place to camp and found a spot far enough from the highway to be hidden from traffic.

The next morning started with a climb. When I reached the crest of the hill I noticed six horses milling around within feet of the highway. I slowly walked past trying not to disturb them. Fifteen minutes later I heard the steady rhythm of hoof beats on pavement. The sound got louder and louder until it was almost startling. The horses looked wild eyed and skittish as they galloped by. Cars were lined up behind them, the drivers not knowing what to do. Ten minutes later a police car stopped and the officer asked if I had seen any horses come by. I pointed straight ahead and wished him luck. After watching way too many TV westerns in my youth I missed my golden opportunity to say: "They went that-a-way!"

By 11:00 am we reached another convenience store. It was a warm day and I purchased an ice cream sandwich. It was so good I went back in and purchased another. We found a shady spot at the side of the store, put down our packs, sat on the pavement, leaned back against the store wall, and enjoyed our food and drink. To a hiker, sitting on the ground is perfectly natural. We do it whenever we take breaks. It feels good to take the weight off of our feet and relax.

To break the monotony of the road walk, Ted, Peggy, and I spent time hiking together and getting to know one another. They are world travelers who have been to countries I didn't even know existed. It was fun hearing about their adventures.

As we were sitting on the pavement eating ice cream, we

were getting curious looks from convenience store customers. I think some of them, particularly the ones who quickly averted their eyes, saw three grimy, deeply tanned, homeless people.

The next thirteen miles to Chama were fairly uneventful. We walked through the tiny town of Tierra Amarilla. That took all of five minutes. I stopped to check out a prairie dog village. Prairie dogs popped their heads out of their dens to check me out, too. I enjoyed watching their chattering, bustling, industriousness. Clouds covered the sky and the wind picked up. I was walking with Ted and Peggy and saw a tiny patch of blue sky far in the distance. I know it was wishful thinking, but I was feeling inspired and started singing: "Blue skies smilin' at me. Nothin' but blue skies do I see. Blue birds singin' a song. Nothin' but blue skies from now on. Never seen the sun shinin' so bright......" I don't think Willie Nelson would have been impressed and Ted and Peggy stared at me like I was crazy, but it was from the heart!

It was wishful thinking, though. We could see Chama and thunderclouds were converging on the little town. Sometimes lightning would come out of the clouds followed by a deep "Boom!" I was glad to finally make it to town and a motel room. We had amazing luck on both days of our road walk and only experienced a few light sprinkles. It could have been a lot worse.

My motel room had a bathtub and I relaxed in the hot soothing water. I met Ted and Peggy an hour later and we headed to the High Country Restaurant. There was a good selection of Mexican food and I ordered the chicken burrito with beans and rice and a beer. The burrito was spicy and good. Half way through the meal I found out it was Peggy's birthday. We had another beer to mark the occasion. No gifts were exchanged but I think she had reason to celebrate. She looked years younger than her actual age, radiated robust health and energy, and had just completed the New Mexico portion of the Continental Divide Trail with a husband who obviously adored her.

I felt like celebrating, too. It was a fun, challenging hike across the length of New Mexico and I was proud of the accomplishment. As a New Mexico resident, I knew the beauty and variety this state had to offer. Hiking the New Mexico section of the Continental Divide Trail exceeded even my expectations.

After an enjoyable dinner we headed back to the motel. Two beers is one past my limit. Once I was in my room I was sound asleep in ten minutes. Pathetic!

7 SOUTH PASS CITY, WYOMING

Snow had accumulated in the San Juan Mountains in May and now the snow level was above average. I have spent most of my life in the New Mexico desert and very little time around snow. I wanted to give the snow plenty of time to melt. Heading to the Great Divide Basin in Wyoming and hiking south from South Pass City, Wyoming to Steamboat Springs, Colorado looked like a viable option. Ted and Peggy agreed and we spent the next day making plans to get there.

Two buses, a taxi, a rental car, another bus, a drive to the Highway 28 trailhead, and three days later we were hiking the three miles from the trailhead to South Pass City. South Pass City is an old gold mining town dating from the 1860's. The gold played out and most of the people left. Eventually it became a ghost town. In recent years some of the abandoned buildings have been restored and it has become a tourist attraction. It is in a lovely grass filled valley with a clear mountain stream running through it. South Pass City is hiker friendly. We stopped at the gift shop and signed the hiker register. They were selling cokes and ice cream which hit the spot. The shop owner couldn't have been nicer. She asked me questions about my pack and light weight backpacking. I had the feeling she was contemplating a thru-hike. I hope she does it. There was no charge to hikers to explore some of the restored buildings so I took a little tour. It gave me a feel for what it was like living in this little town 150 years ago. Interesting place. Friendly people.

Leaving South Pass City we followed Willow Creek for a mile then started a steep climb into the mountains. We hiked through pine forest for the next three hours with challenging climbs, steep descents, and great views. Eventually we came out of the mountains and the terrain turned to rolling hills. For the rest of the day it was rocky cross country hiking from cairn to cairn. In the afternoon I saw my first of many pronghorn antelope. I had been looking forward to this moment since I began planning my CDT hike. It was about one hundred feet away and seemed more curious than frightened.

We reached the Sweetwater River by 7:00 pm and camped in a grassy area beside the river. I always tried to place my tent far enough from Ted and Peggy that I couldn't hear their conversation and they couldn't hear my snoring. After setting up our tents, Ted always invited me to have dinner with them. It was an enjoyable time to relax and unwind. After dinner I headed to the river to fill my water bottles. I was next to a small bridge and beneath the bridge there were dozens of mud covered swallow nests. As I was filling the bottles, swallows swarmed overhead. It looked like an air traffic controller's worst nightmare. Time after time they would come within a millisecond of impact; then dart in different directions.

That night I slept like a log. I love sleeping next to rivers and streams. To me, they are Nature's sleeping pills. Unfortunately, Ted and Peggy didn't have the same experience. The zipper on their tent wasn't working and by the next morning twelve ticks had invaded their tent.

This was the day we entered the Great Divide Basin. I knew nothing about it beforehand. In my mind it was going to be an easy, flat, 118 mile hike on dirt roads to Rawlins, Wyoming. It was a basin, wasn't it? Was I pleasantly mistaken! Hiking the Great Divide Basin was one of the highlights of my journey. It was far from flat. The best way to describe it is vast and isolated. We didn't see any hikers in the five days we travelled through the basin and only a handful of vehicles and people.

Most of the first day was just what I was expecting. Every direction I looked there was nothing but flat treeless sage covered ground. The Trail followed dirt roads for miles in a straight line. Navigation was easy, which was a pleasure. There was a smell of sage in the air. I walked by patches of phlox with their delicate white petals and wonderful smell. The combination of the two aromas was intoxicating. At times the CDT was on the old Oregon Trail. I could visualize covered wagons rolling along the rutted dirt road and hear the crack of a whip.

Since we were on a road we could walk side by side. Ted and Peggy had vacationed in an amazing number of countries and shared some of their adventures. I am not a world traveler and it was fun to vicariously travel to China, stay at farm houses in South Africa, and take an African Safari. Later in the day rolling hills and an occasional arroyo started to appear. The wind picked up and we were getting wind-whipped. The sound of the wind rushing by my ears made it difficult to hear conversations. That evening we found a place to camp in a steep walled, sandy arroyo that provided some protection from the wind. We hiked a respectable twenty-two miles and it wasn't difficult.

On day two the flat easy hiking I was expecting all the way to Rawlins disappeared. All day the wind was powerful and unrelenting. It was cold and stayed cold. I put on my rain jacket and tightened the hood to shield my ears from the constant bombardment of the LOUD wind. It wasn't the force of the wind that was the problem, it was the never ending Noise!

At noon we stopped for lunch behind tall rocks that served as a windbreak. It was a pleasure to talk in a normal voice for a change. We were on top of a mesa looking far down to a huge valley. Straight ahead were tall flat topped hills three miles in the distance. To our left, the valley continued to the horizon. To our right and hundreds of feet below was a rugged canyon filled valley at least ten miles wide extending as far as I could see.

Ted and Peggy finished their break and I watched them descend to the valley. There was a ridge that divided the upper and lower valley and I could see them follow the ridge line and eventually head up the hill. I was in no hurry to fight the wind so from my sheltered perch I watched Ted and Peggy get smaller and smaller. By the time they were half way up the hill they were tiny. When they neared the top I had to focus on a small area and look for movement. Once I saw movement I knew it was them. Finally, two tiny objects reached the peak of the hill and vanished. I figured I had better get going. I didn't want to leave. This place filled me with good vibrations. One last look at the magnificent views and it was time to head out.

The sky was a deep blue. Listed water sources actually had water but after the New Mexico desert I still carried four quarts just to be sure. I noticed a big pile of fresh horse droppings and heard movement. Up the hill and to my right five wild horses were staring at me from less than one hundred feet away. The grey stallion seemed curious and moved a little closer. Five minutes later they effortlessly galloped through the dense sage and crossed the pathway fifty feet in front of me. It was unexpected and exciting. An hour later I saw eight horses grazing on a far ridge. A couple of them were silhouetted against the blue sky. They looked strong, independent, and majestic. They looked wild.

Later in the day I caught up to Ted and Peggy. Rain clouds were forming. We were nearing the top of a hill and heading toward dark virga. There were small patches of clear sky, but not many. I heard Peggy start to sing softly: "Blue skies shinin' on me....." Then Ted joined in: "Nothin' but blue skies do I see...." Then I joined in: "Bluebirds singin' a song...." Then we continued together: "Nothin but blue skies from now on. Never seen the sun shinin' so bright...." Three hopeful optimists were walking side by side, laughing, and singing miserably off key. It is one of my fondest CDT memories.

In the evening we descended almost 1,000 feet to a wide valley then headed east for a mile to a great little stream where we camped. What a fun day! We hiked twenty- two and a half miles and I was beat.

Day three was spent walking on ranch and gas pipeline roads across sage covered cattle country. We were many miles from towns and highways. It was easy hiking and we covered twenty-five and a half miles. I was right in my element and loving it. Hiking through this isolated land I was far from the hustle and bustle and stress of civilization. I didn't carry an I-phone, I-pad, I-pod, Kindle, or any other form of human distraction. Hiking along the dusty road I could smell the sage, feel the wind hit my body, watch the clouds changing shape, feel the warmth of the sun, have relaxed, unhurried conversations with Ted and Peggy, scan the landscape for pronghorn antelope, daydream, feel my fit body easily handle the three miles an hour pace, quench my thirst with cold well water, tuck down into a little culvert and join Ted and Peggy for lunch, hear the wind howling overhead, and thoroughly enjoy living in the moment.

By 7:00 pm we started looking for a camping spot. The sage was so tightly spaced there was not enough room to put a tent. We searched for a half an hour before heading up a small ranch road and finding a couple of spots just big enough for our tents. As we were putting up the tents a little pronghorn antelope watched us from the top of a nearby hill. I could see its silhouette against the twilight sky. We were out in the middle of nowhere. After dark, stars filled the sky. It was quiet and peaceful. Before long I was sound asleep.

On day four we continued hiking on the gas pipeline road. It was windy but what else was new? That was just part of hiking the Great Divide Basin. In six miles we steeply descended to a wide valley and walked by picnic tables and restrooms located next to a couple of alkaline ponds. I was glad I still had plenty of water. Six miles later we started walking on a seldom used paved road. We could see Highway 287 leading to Rawlins far in the distance. The paved road had so little use I was walking on the road instead of the apron. I was daydreaming when I turned around and saw a huge dust devil heading right at me. It was twenty feet away and moving fast. I grabbed my hat and prepared to get hit. I was immediately encased in swirling, stinging sand and literally swept across the road, the apron, and down an eight foot embankment. I had absolutely no control. Once I reached the embankment I took four quick steps then dug my heels into the dirt and slid the rest of the way to the bottom. I managed to stay upright, but I was stunned! All I could say was: "Holy Shit!" It only lasted five seconds but it was swift and shocking! Ted and Peggy were ahead of me and hit by the dust devil, too. Our adrenaline was pumping for quite some time.

In a couple of miles we reached Highway 287. We were facing traffic on the busy four lane highway and fighting a nasty headwind. There had been so little human contact since leaving South Pass City it was a shock having loud cars and trucks barreling by just feet away. After a twenty-three mile day we made it to an excellent campsite on the west side of Nine Mile Hill. You rarely camp at an established campsite on the Continental Divide Trail. This was a real treat. We put our tents on soft level ground that had seen much use over the years. We were about a half mile from the highway but Nine Mile Hill blocked most of the traffic noise. We were well positioned to reach Rawlins by noon and looking forward to a zero day.

8 RAWLINS, WYOMING

We were moving with alacrity the next morning. Four miles before town we ran into Trail Magic. It was cases of Mountain Dew, Coke, and Root Beer. We took pictures holding the cases and beaming! This was my first Trail Magic the whole trip. I opted for the Mountain Dew. It tasted great!

CDT Marmot and Trail Dog

Make that the second Trail Magic. The first Trail Magic was the gallon jug of water in the New Mexico desert when I was in desperate need. Ted and Peggy were the Trail Angels who filled that jug and left it when they hiked through a day earlier. I thanked them profusely when I found out.

We made it to town and headed to Buck's Sports Grill. It felt good to sit down in a cushioned booth, drink a tall glass of iced tea, relax, and people watch. The food was filling and when we finished we headed across town to the La Bella Motel. Ted and Peggy had forwarded a resupply box to the La Bella and that's where we planned to spend the night. There was only one room left at the motel and Ted and Peggy generously let me have it. They went in search of another motel while I checked in. I was given a cordial greeting by Mary, the owner, and her little dog Charlie. After checking in I headed to my room and straight to the shower. It had been too long and felt good to be clean again. Ted and Peggy were going to drop by my room at 6:00 pm and until then I had a chance to lie down on the comfortable bed, watch TV, and get off of my feet.

They arrived right on time and we headed next door to the Big City Bar & Grill. They specialized in steaks but also had a good selection of Mexican food. Peggy ordered, then I ordered the huevos rancheros with sopapillas, and Ted ordered the combination plate with unlimited refills. The place had a nice feel to it. We drank our beers and chatted. Finally the food arrived and looked delicious. It was. I fancy myself a connoisseur of Mexican food. I eat it every chance I get and have for the past fifty years. This was damned good! The cook was talented! I demolished my huevos rancheros then took my time savoring the light, flaky, sopapillas covered with honey. Yum! Ted finished his unlimited combination plate and ordered two more tacos. The huevos rancheros were excellent but I was really jealous when those two tacos arrived at the table. Ted seemed to be enjoying them way too much. I let out a little whimper and he laughed! A cruel laugh! After an enjoyable dinner we headed back to our rooms. I felt relaxed and ready for a good night's sleep.

I awoke refreshed the next morning. I remembered that I had only asked for one night's stay at the motel instead of two and hurried over to the office. There was a little table set up with coffee and trail bars. Mary signed me up for another day. I had gotten the last room available. We chatted for a while. She was a nice lady. Honest, too. Yogi's CDT Guide had the La Bella Motel listed as $45 a night and that is what Mary charged. This was the height of tourist season. The town was full of energy extraction workers needing a place to stay. Demand for rooms far exceeded supply. The La Bella's rooms weren't fancy, but they were spacious, clean, had wi-fi, and a 25" flat screen TV. The La Bella was American owned and had received the AARP Five Star Award. Mary could have charged double the room rate and gotten it. This honest, unassuming lady charged $45 plus tax. That spoke volumes about her character. The coffee was good, too.

It was a chilly, blustery, rainy day and I was glad not to be hiking. In fact, I just wanted to be lazy. I spent the day watching TV, napping, and relaxing. I met my friends for dinner and headed back to the Big City Bar & Grill. This time I knew what to order – the unlimited combination plate. I had been waiting all day for this. It didn't disappoint. I went after the tacos, enchiladas, chile rellenos, Spanish rice and pinto beans with a vengeance. They were excellent. I asked for a refill of everything except the chile rellenos. Excellent! Excellent! Excellent! I was stuffed! A beer to wash it down and I was good to go.

I was well rested and fortified from my stay in Rawlins and eager to start the eighty-three mile journey to Riverside, Wyoming. Leaving Rawlins, we hiked the first twelve miles through canyons, along a draw, through more canyons and arroyos, and up a steep hill before stopping for lunch. We could see a small highway a mile in the distance. Ted and Peggy planned to hike over to the highway and take a more direct route to Riverside. I planned to take the Bear Creek route. In forty-five miles my route would join their highway and I would start looking for their shoe prints. I wasn't sure if I would be able to catch them before Riverside but I was going to try. It felt kind of strange watching them head away. We had been hiking together for many miles.

I hiked from cairn to cairn the next four miles before reaching Bridger Pass Road and followed the well maintained gravel road the rest of the day. It was easy hiking and the views were panoramic. The only drawback was a constant thirty mile an hour wind.

Bridger Pass Road travelled through a wide grass filled valley with cattle grazing in the fields. It reminded me of the rolling hills and green valleys of Virginia. Far in the distance the steep walled Atlantic Rim enclosed the west side of the valley. On the east side the valley gradually changed to gently sloping hills. It seemed like every fifteen minutes I would see a pronghorn antelope grazing in the fields.

There were huge isolated ranches. Only three pickups and a cattle truck drove by the whole time I was hiking along the road. A couple of the ranchers glowered instead of waved.

Barbed wire enclosed the properties. No Trespassing signs were frequent. I had the feeling the ranchers were serious. The only option was to cowboy camp in the narrow area between the fence and road. I picked up my pace to see if I could make it to Muddy Creek and find a better place to camp. It would mean a thirty-three mile day but it looked like my best option.

By evening the wind was down to a cool breeze, crickets were chirping, and the hiking was quite pleasant. It was almost dark by the time I reached Muddy Creek. I was delighted to see a good flow of clear, clean water. I was expecting muddy. It was a nice night and I set up my tent with just the netting. I slept uncovered on top of my air mattress. At 1:00 in the morning I felt moisture hitting me. I looked up and the sky was full of stars. So much condensation was coming from the creek it almost felt like a mist. Once I realized it wasn't rain I went back to sleep. Before falling asleep I could hear a coyote howling at the moon. I love that lonely sound.

Everything was saturated with condensation the next morning. I was packed up and hiking just as it was getting light enough to see. I crossed over a cattle guard, entered private ranch land, and caught up to ten cows grazing next to the road. Once they noticed me they started trotting down the road. They would stop, stare at me with a blank look, wait for me to catch up, and start trotting down the road again. This happened over and over. It was getting frustrating. I decided to have some breakfast and give the cattle a chance to scatter. I sat down in a culvert beside the road and leaned back against its side. Oatmeal and raisins were on the menu and tasted good. From my field of view I could see miles of green rolling pasture land and some of the bluest sky on the planet. I finished breakfast and headed on my way. Five minutes later I caught up to the same freaking cows! It was like they were waiting for me so we could continue the game: "Get on the road. Trot. Trot. Trot. Stop. Blank stare. Wait for me to catch up. Trot. Trot. Trot." Aaaarrrgggg! More cows were actually starting to accumulate in front of me. I could see a fence and cattle guard in the distance. When we reached the cattle guard the cows FINALLY scattered.

As I was writing this an annoying question kept nagging me. I tried to ignore it but it wouldn't go away. "Why didn't you just get off of the road, hike around the cows, and get back on the road once you passed them?" I tried to remember if there were any obstacles to keep me from doing this. There weren't. Hmmm.....The only conclusion I could reach: I wasn't any brighter than the cows!

There was some great hiking the next eighteen miles with challenging climbs and descents and fantastic views from mountaintops. Far on the horizon were tall snowcapped mountains and it looked like the CDT was heading right at them.

In the afternoon I reached the highway that Ted and Peggy were travelling. I followed it for two miles then turned onto a dirt road that headed to the mountains. Within a half mile I spotted their shoe prints and within a mile I was back in the forest. I stopped at a mountain stream and filled my bottles with the cold refreshing water. This was difficult hiking. There was a cross country climb through briar patches and brambles and another long bushwhacking climb through thick forest. By the time I reached the top I was running out of steam. It was 7:30 pm and I had hiked thirty-one miles. I planned on hiking until 8:00 pm to see if I could catch up to Ted and Peggy but I turned a corner and there they were. They had finished hiking only minutes earlier and were starting to set up their tent. What a pleasant surprise. They were just as surprised to see me. We set up our tents and shared our adventures over dinner.

It felt good to be back in the mountains. We had a steep climb to start the day and hiked through open fields, dense forest, and lush green meadows. Elk were grazing in one of the meadows. I was hoping to hear an elk bugling, but no luck.

A couple of hours later we were at the base of the snowcapped mountains I had seen the day before. We started a long climb through a beautiful pine forest. The air was thick with the smell of pine and rich earth. Sparkling mountain streams began to show up. We took our first break near a small patch of snow. We weren't very high on the mountain and snow was already starting to show up? I had a feeling this was going to be a looong day.

After our break we continued to climb. Snow patches were becoming more frequent and thicker. Soon most of the ground was covered in snow. After a while the pathway faded and we began to rely on the GPS for direction. The snow became thicker and our footing less stable. I would look at my GPS and point the direction. Ted took the initiative and broke trail through the snow. I followed his footsteps. I could tell he had a lot of experience hiking in snow. He tried to keep us in the shadows where the snow was firmer and he stayed away from the base of trees whenever possible. Breaking trail was hard and I could hear him go "Ooofff!" when he would suddenly posthole. After an hour I decided to give him a break and take the lead. I quickly realized how much skill was involved and how much I lacked. I came too close to the base of a small tree and in an instant my right leg dropped down into the snow all the way to my hip. It jolted my body! I tried to lift my leg out but it wouldn't budge. My mind wanted to panic but I could tell my leg wasn't injured and I could take my time and figure a way out. Ted came over to give me a hand. He didn't say anything but I could read his mind: "Rookie!" Ted went back to breaking trail.

Our first goal was to reach Bridger Peak and at 11,007 feet we had our work cut out for us. Once we reached Bridger Peak, it would be four miles down to Battle Pass and a 15 mile hitch to Riverside.

For the next few hours I got a lesson from Ted and Peggy on how to hike in snow. It was tiring and took a lot of focus and I wouldn't admit it to them until we made it to Battle Pass, but I was having a ball! I was hiking in deep snow through a fragrant forest thick with spruce and pine. At my home in Rio Rancho, New Mexico on June 21st the temperature was probably 99 degrees.

A half mile before Bridger Peak we came out of the trees and followed a wide patch of snow covered ground the rest of the way to the peak. Peggy was in the lead in this section. The snow was firm enough that she could glide over the top. I followed her footsteps in the snow. Whenever her footsteps went down in the snow a few inches I would be prepared to posthole and sometimes did. Ted brought up the rear and with his heavier body I could hear him postholing often.

Dark clouds were moving in and looked like they would meet us just when we reached Bridger Peak. There was an occasional rumble of thunder. We were in an exposed area near the top of the mountain. It was an uncomfortable feeling. We had to figure out if we needed to backtrack to the trees and give the clouds a chance to move through, or follow the CDT as it passed Bridger Peak and headed down a wide valley. There were trees at the side of the valley where we could find shelter. We opted to follow the Trail down the valley, angled over to the trees, and took a break. We had been so focused on the hike it was the first break we had taken in hours. Within half an hour the clouds were no longer a threat.

9 RIVERSIDE, WYOMING

Going down the valley I watched Peggy slide over five foot snowbanks and keep her balance. It looked fun so I tried it. It was fun. We soon headed back into the dense forest, relied heavily on the GPS, and were fortunate enough to have Ted lead the way. I would be ten or twenty feet behind him reading my GPS and giving instructions: "Head more to the left. Good. Now go straight." As we descended below snow level we eventually hit a wide path that led to Battle Pass. By the time we reached the highway it was almost dark and we were weary hikers. The hitch from Battle Pass was supposed to be difficult but we were lucky to get a quick ride to town. A nice couple and their grandson dropped us off at the Lazy Acres Campground and Motel. There were no motel rooms available so we set up our tents. By now it was 9:00 pm but we were hungry and headed across the street to the Bear Trap Café. The restaurant had just closed but the kind owner saw three bedraggled hikers took pity on us and let us order dinner. After dinner, the friendly waitress even gave each of us a decadent piece of chocolate cake for free. Such a thoughtful owner and waitress. Thank you.

I figured I would easily fall asleep but I was too wound up from the events of the day. It was such a strenuous hike I was too tired to sleep. My tent was close to the main road and I could hear cars driving by. There was a bar across the street and when the bar closed I could hear the patron's conversations as they headed to their vehicles. It was 2:00 in the morning before I finally wound down enough to sleep. We were planning to take a zero day so I slept in a little the next morning.

I joined Ted and Peggy at the Bear Trap Café for breakfast and we discussed plans for the next leg of our journey to Steamboat Springs, Colorado. There was still a lot of snow in the mountains between Battle Pass and Steamboat Springs so we decided to road walk. We planned a two day road walk to Walden, Colorado and another two days to reach Highway 40 and a hitch to Steamboat Springs.

After breakfast we took down our tents and moved to motel rooms when they became available. The Lazy Acres Motel was quite nice and the owners went out of their way to be helpful and friendly. I was still sore from the previous day and my motel room had a bathtub. I made the water so hot I had to inch my way into the tub but it was just what my tired aching muscles needed.

I had hiked thirty-three, thirty-one, and a very strenuous nineteen miles the previous three days. My hiker appetite was in full force and I did some heavy duty eating at lunch and dinner. We all did. An excellent night's sleep and I was recovered and ready to go the next morning.

I expected the walk along the highway to be a drag, but it wasn't. Wyoming is the tenth biggest state in land volume and has the fewest people of any state in the nation. The walk showcased its blue unpolluted skies and wide open spaces. We passed multi-building ranches on huge tracts of land. This was cattle country and we passed herds of cattle. Far on the horizon were snowcapped mountains.

Part of my every day routine was to watch the movement of the clouds as they crossed the sky. It was a challenge trying to figure out which way the clouds were flowing and if they would intercept our path. By the end of the day there were dark clouds ahead and we looked to be on a collision course. We came to a wide swiftly flowing stream. Near the stream were places to put our tents. It was only 6:00 pm but I was ready to bail. We did. We just got sprinkled on and I was glad we stopped when we did.

We hiked twenty-eight miles to Walden, Colorado the next day. Shortly after entering Colorado the highway made a long climb. When we reached the top we entered a vast open plain probably thirty miles wide and forty miles long called North Park. The land was dotted with ranches. I looked for Walden but it was so far away I couldn't see it. Eventually I could see a bump on the horizon. The bump became bigger and started to take on the outline of a town. It looked an agonizingly far distance away. Mentally, I have found it better if I can't see my destination. This was like coming into Grants, New Mexico all over. Fortunately we were on an undulating highway and there were only occasional glimpses of Walden. Once we were within five miles of town we had another race with a thunderstorm. We had already hiked twenty-three miles and now we had to hike at top speed against a heavy wind the last five miles. We made it to Walden and headed straight to the nearest motel. As we were signing in the rain started pouring. All the extra effort paid off. It was very satisfying listening to that rain. The booming thunder was icing on the cake.

Leaving Walden my legs ached from the twenty-eight mile day. The area was still mainly ranch land but diversity was starting to show up. I hiked past miles of irrigated farm land, a dairy with a huge herd of cattle and massive haystacks, a field full of bulls, oil fields with pump jacks slowly moving up and down, and a new oil well being drilled.

The highlight of the day had to be when we watched two massive bulls get into a fight. They were bellowing and dust was flying everywhere. The dominant bull actually pushed the other bull over the barbed wire fence. Ouch! Now this massive angry bull was thirty feet from us on our side of the fence. We tried to ever so quietly pass by, hoping he wouldn't notice us. I felt sorry for the defeated bull. He looked humiliated and stunned. Fortunately he was still focused on the other bull and didn't pay any attention to us.

By the end of the day we were weary hikers. We had been trying to find a place to camp for the last hour with no luck. We reached the top of a hill and found a great camping spot on open land. Looking out from our campsite there was a beautiful valley below surrounded by aspen and pines. Tall mountains acted as a backdrop. Elk quietly grazed in the valley. We set up our tents and fixed our dinner. We knew this might be the last dinner together on the Trail and it couldn't have been in a better location. As always we had plenty to talk about. I genuinely enjoyed Ted and Peggy's company. They were appreciators. It's fun to be around appreciators. They weren't afraid to say: "Look at that sunset. Isn't it beautiful?" "Look at those gorgeous aspen!" "Can you believe this view?

Wow!"

When we reached Steamboat Springs they would be heading back to their home in Seattle. Ted had a board meeting he needed to attend. They planned to resume their hike on the 19th of July.

I would be heading home, too. I wanted to give the snow in the South San Juan Mountains more time to melt. Once I was home I would keep a close eye on the snow levels and decide the best time to head back to Chama, New Mexico and resume my hike north.

10 STEAMBOAT SPRINGS, COLORADO

The next morning we followed Highway 14 until we reached Highway 40. Now it was a matter of getting a hitch to Steamboat Springs. There was plenty of traffic but it was moving fast. We moved further up the highway to find a better location. Still no luck. We were walking to another location when a weather beaten little car screeched to a halt beside us. Its left wheels were still partially on the highway and a big truck had to swerve to miss it. We very quickly hopped in. The driver was a gregarious young man in his mid-twenties who was about as close to a "free spirit" as I have ever been around. He was heading to a Rainbow Family of Living get together in Utah with 10,000 other free spirits. He had never been employed and had no plans to be employed in the foreseeable future. His car was his home.

As we were driving along the winding mountain road I noticed the front right side of the car was shimmying and brought it to his attention. "Don't mind that. My regular tire busted a few days ago and I'm using the spare." He was taking the steep curves at 55 miles an hour. The maximum recommended speed for those little donut tires is 45 miles an hour. I mentioned it to him. He looked at me with a gleam in his eyes and increased the speed to 60. It was a white knuckle ride down the mountains to Steamboat Springs. I breathed a big sigh of relief when I stepped out of that car. We chipped in $20 for gas and wished him luck.

Our destination was the Rabbit Ears Motel. The helpful, knowledgeable, motel manager assigned us rooms and after cleaning up we got together to explore Steamboat Springs, Colorado. I always wanted to visit Steamboat Springs just because of its intriguing name. It is a tourist town with lots of interesting shops and tons of restaurants. This was June 27th the height of tourist season and the main street was crowded with people. It felt weird being around so many people.

We had an enjoyable dinner at an Italian Restaurant but in a way it was kind of sad knowing tomorrow we would be heading our separate ways. I consider Ted and Peggy friends.

I am a solitary hiker. When I started hiking with them I figured it would last three days at the most. We ended up hiking twenty-six days and almost 400 miles together. One of my fondest memories is of the many hours we walked along talking about anything and everything. I hope we can do it again in the future.

Ted and Peggy did resume their hike on July 19th and headed north from South Pass City, Wyoming. They finished Wyoming and part of Montana before stopping short of the Canadian border. In 2015 they hiked 400 more miles in Montana to the Canadian border. They still need to finish the section between Steamboat Springs and Chama, New Mexico to complete their CDT hike and plan to do that in 2016.

I made it home a couple of days later and got an enthusiastic greeting from my beagle, Fred. It felt good to be back and give my weary body a chance to recuperate. I was in peak physical condition but the snow level in the South San Juan Mountains was still more than I wanted to deal with. Once I determined the snow levels were acceptable I headed back to Chama. I spent two days in the gorgeous South San Juan Mountains. The views were amazing. This was tough hiking at high altitude. I only made thirty miles in those two days and had weeks of mountain hiking ahead of me. I realized I had waited too long for the snow to melt and wouldn't make it to the Canadian border before the snows hit. My CDT thru-hike was over. Continental Divide Trail – 1   Jim Hill – 0. The instant I made the decision to end the hike there was a feeling of relief followed by a determination to get it right the next time. My mind immediately started working on a plan for a successful thru-hike. I don't remember feeling overly disappointed. It had been a fun hike that left me with great memories and I learned a lot from my attempt. I definitely want a rematch.

11 HOW I PLAN TO THRU-HIKE THE CONTINENTAL DIVIDE TRAIL AT AGE 69

I thru-hiked the Appalachian Trail in 2009, the Pacific Crest Trail in 2012, and hiked 980 miles of the Continental Divide Trail in 2014. From those hikes I have gained experience that has improved my hiking efficiency even as I get older and slower. Through trial and error I have learned what works and doesn't work for me. When I find something that works, I stick with it. I plan to thru-hike the Continental Divide Trail in 2016. The route I have chosen will be 2,850 miles. That's a long way. I need to use my experience to maximize my enjoyment, minimize the wear and tear on my body, and successfully complete the hike.

Here's how I plan to do it.

Hiking the Continental Divide Trail

Scott Williamson set speed records hiking the Pacific Crest Trail and was the first person to yo-yo the PCT. One of the many things that impressed me about him was that he kept his hike simple. He put his pack on his back and followed the Trail in one direction from border to border.

As a hiker in his sixties I want to see if I can do that too. I kept it simple on my Appalachian Trail and Pacific Crest Trail thru-hikes and I am proud of that. I want to do the same hiking the Continental Divide Trail.

Whether I hike northbound from Mexico to Canada or southbound from Canada to Mexico I will follow an unbroken footpath and hike only in one direction. I will follow the Bear Creek route and use his maps including his alternate trail maps. If I hike an alternate trail it will be because it is the more beautiful route and not to make my hike easier. If there are thunderstorms ahead I will wait for the storms to pass and not take a lower route around the mountains. If I have to take a fire detour, I will. If I get bogged down by snow that is more than I can handle, I will stop and wait for snow conditions to improve. I will stay on the Bear Creek trail. I will not detour around the snow or skip to another area. When I hike my pack stays on my back.

Hiking Style

One day while I was hiking the Pacific Crest Trail I kept getting passed by a thru-hiker called Freestyle. When he caught up to me for the fourth time he said: "You are like a metronome, Jim. You steadily move down the Trail." Metronome probably should have been my trail name. Moving steadily down the Trail is what helped me complete the Pacific Crest Trail and that's the way I plan to thru-hike the Continental Divide Trail.

When I started my first thru-hike on the Appalachian Trail I was in good physical condition and competitive. I wanted to see if I could hike the Trail in four months. Within the first week I was trying to hike twenty plus mile days. I liked to pass people. I pushed myself hard and by the time I reached

Kent, Connecticut I was still on schedule to complete the Trail in four months. That competitive drive was wearing me down and taking the fun out of hiking. Kent, Connecticut is when I slowed my hike down and enjoyed it much more. When I slowed my pace I noticed I had more energy and just felt better. Out of habit I continued hiking ten hour days. Even with the slower pace the amount of miles I hiked each day surprised me. I reached Mt. Katahdin on September 22nd with time to spare before the snow.

Lesson learned: Hiking a consistent number of hours each day at a steady pace = a surprising number of miles and a much more enjoyable hike.

I took that idea with me to the Pacific Crest Trail. My plan was to hike from 7:30 in the morning to 7:30 at night with fifteen minute food breaks every two hours. That would allow for a solid ten hours of actual hiking. I planned a pace where my speed would adjust to the terrain - 2 miles an hour or less on uphills, 2.5 - 3 miles an hour at normal speed. I rarely pushed the pace. Hiking from 7:30 am to 7:30 pm also gave me at least eleven hours off of my feet so I could get plenty of rest. I was much less competitive on this hike and quite content to be passed by other hikers. I kept up with many of the younger hikers for over a thousand miles. It would be hard to count the number of times they passed me. Hiking from 7:30 am to 7:30 pm worked like a charm. I hiked the Appalachian Trail in 148 days and the Pacific Crest Trail in 149 days. The Pacific Crest Trail is 482 miles longer than the Appalachian Trail. Because of the more relaxed pace I had much more energy hiking the Pacific Crest Trail which led to a very enjoyable hike and a quick recovery once I finished. With less stress on my body I didn't need to take as many zero days to recuperate. I much preferred nero days. I tried to get to town by noon which gave me plenty of time to take care of town chores, relax, eat plenty of food, and get a good night's sleep.

Lesson learned: Hiking from 7:30 am to 7:30 pm works like a charm. Keep doing it.

I continued hiking from 7:30 am to 7:30 pm on the Continental Divide Trail but I tweaked it. While I was hiking I tried for a comfortable pace - a relaxed pace with no extra effort involved. If I felt myself straining I slowed down. I might be hiking at 1.5 miles an hour on a steep uphill, three miles an hour on a dirt road, paved highway, or smooth even pathway, and 2.5 miles an hour in between. If I felt any strain I slowed down. My mantra was "relaxed, smooth, effortless". The "relaxed, smooth, effortless" mentality took the stress away and allowed me to relax and enjoy my surroundings as I was hiking. That worked really well. It also gave me the miles I was looking for each day and was much easier on my body. I had energy to spare while hiking 980 miles of the Continental Divide Trail. It was so effective, I reached Chama, New Mexico and the snow covered San Juan Mountains four days earlier than I planned.

Lesson learned: Hiking from 7:30 am to 7:30 pm with the "relaxed, smooth, effortless" tweak works even better.

Sleep

Getting a good night's sleep gives my older body a chance to recharge. It made a big difference in the quality of my Pacific Crest Trail hike. Many times I ended the day a weary hiker and started the next morning fresh and ready to go. Hiking from 7:30 am to 7:30 pm gave me twelve hours to recuperate from the day's hike. After putting up the tent, eating, adding up my daily mileage, checking my maps to see what was on the agenda for the next day, and recording the day's events on my calendar, I almost always turned off my headlamp by 9:00 pm. I slept from 9:00 pm to 6:00 am. Nine hours of good solid rejuvenating sleep. I listened closely to my body. If I was tired and needed extra sleep I would sleep until I felt like getting up. A couple of times I slept twelve solid hours. Many times I slept ten hours. I've never had colds or been physically ill while hiking. Giving my body a chance to recharge with a good deep sleep is probably one of the reasons why.

I try to create a comfortable sleeping environment. I always sleep in my sturdy, wind and rain resistant Big Agnes Seedhouse SL1 tent where I am screened from mosquitoes, flies, ants, and bugs of any kind. I sleep on a thick, comfortable Therm-a-Rest Neo Air Mattress which keeps me above lumpy ground and other irritants. I use a down sleeping bag for warmth and comfort which becomes a quilt in the summer months.

Lesson learned: A bug free good night's sleep on a comfortable air mattress = a happier more energetic hiker.

Food

On the Appalachian Trail I started stoveless and changed to hot foods by Virginia. I never got the hang of either. I haven't eaten a tortilla with peanut butter or a Lipton Noodle dinner with salmon since 2009.

I knew I needed to make changes on my Pacific Crest Trail hike. My main staple was a trail mix consisting of Shreaded Wheat squares, granola, raisins, dried apples, dried apricots, dried bananas, sunflower seeds, mixed nuts, peanuts, and almonds. I started each morning with Pop Tarts and Nutella spread over bagels. This combination of foods gave me the energy I needed and I didn't get tired of it. I took fifteen minute food breaks every two hours which supplied my body with an even flow of energy throughout the day.

When I reached Sisters, Oregon I was weary after days of difficult hiking. I resupplied at an employee owned grocery store. The prices were incredible and I bought way more food than I needed. I decided to eat as much as I could each time I took a break just so I could get rid of the excess pack weight. Day after day I kept piling the food into my body. Before going to bed I would eat until I was completely full. Often it was a massive amount. I didn't eat anything sugary before going to bed. As I slept I was using that extra food to rebuild muscle broken down by the day's hike and refuel for the day ahead. My energy levels picked up dramatically and I lost the little layer of fatigue that had been following me around for too long. I thought: "Hmmm. Maybe I'm onto something." From then on each time I resupplied I carried an extra day of food and made sure I finished all of the food by the time I reached the next resupply town. I wanted to be eating as much while I was hiking as I did when I was pigging out in town. It worked. I continued carrying the extra day of food all the way to Canada.

The trail mix was hard crunchy food and I broke a tooth 1,000 miles into the hike. I needed to find foods that were lightweight, nutritious, calorie dense, yet soft enough not to break my teeth. On the Continental Divide Trail the two main foods I relied on were dehydrated pinto beans and regular oatmeal. They were lightweight yet filled with calories and nutrition. I included raisins, powdered milk, cinnamon, shelled sunflower seeds, ketchup, Idahoan potatoes, and stove top stuffing in my diet. I enjoyed the oatmeal right from the start and once I got my hiker appetite I enjoyed the pinto beans. Sometimes I would combine the beans with Idahoan Potatoes, ketchup, and raisins. Stovetop stuffing and beans with ketchup and raisins tasted good, too. I alternated between the pinto beans and oatmeal throughout the day and they hydrated as I was hiking. It took a couple of hours for the oatmeal to hydrate and three hours for the pinto beans. I would take a fifteen minute food break every three hours when I ate the pinto beans and every two hours for the oatmeal. Once the food was hydrated it filled the twenty-four ounce Gatorade container all the way to the top and by the time I finished eating I was full. Before going to bed I ate an extra amount of food until I was completely full. My diet worked. It gave me energy to spare. I will use the dehydrated beans and oatmeal on my 2016 CDT thru-hike.

Lesson learned: The dehydrated pinto beans and oatmeal work. Eating as much each day hiking as I would in town gives me energy to spare. Taking fifteen minute food breaks every two to three hours gives me a chance to relax and supplies my body with an even flow of energy throughout the day.

Planning

I spent twice as much time planning for the Continental Divide Trail hike as I did for the Pacific Crest Trail and Appalachian Trail hikes. I knew this was going to be a tough hike and I wanted to be as prepared as possible. I purchased "Yogi's Continental Divide Trail Handbook". It was excellent. I don't know how many times I said "Thank you, Yogi." while I was planning my hike and when I was actually hiking the CDT. It was a lot!

I used Bear Creek's maps in conjunction with his GPS waypoints for navigation and they did an outstanding job keeping me oriented. I purchased all five Bear Creek Mapbooks - New Mexico, Colorado, Wyoming, Montana, and Popular Alternate Routes. I also bought the Jonathan Ley maps and followed Yogi's "Map Recommendations". When the two maps overlapped I wrote with a magic marker the more detailed Ley notes onto the Bear Creek maps. The Ley notes were especially useful for water information.

The Bear Creek maps were printed front and back. I numbered each page starting with Page 1 at the Crazy Cook trailhead to Page 348 at the northern terminus in Waterton Park, Canada. My goal was to fill pages 1 to 348 with all the information I needed so it was right at my fingertips.

On page one I had written: "1st Resupply – Lordsburg, 85 Miles, Approx 5 Days, 13.7 Miles to 1st Water Box". On Page 4 – "Water Box #2 Just Before A Fence Crossing, 19 Miles To Next Water Box-Load Up".

When my map showed a highway leading to a resupply town I would draw an arrow along the highway in the direction of the town and the give the distance to the town. I would staple a page from Yogi's Town Guide onto the map. The front page had the name of the town, Post Office, grocery stores, laundry, campgrounds, and more, plus the phone numbers and hours each were open. Motels were listed with their rates and hiker friendly motels earned a happy face. On the back of the page was a map showing the location of the Post Office, motels, grocery stores, restaurants, etc.

Once I left a resupply town and was back on the Trail my

map gave the name of the next resupply town and the distance to it. In areas where water was crucial I underlined water sources and gave the distance between sources.

Lesson learned: I tried to have all my planning done before I started my hike so I could focus on hiking.

Navigation

The Appalachian Trail and the Pacific Crest Trail were both clearly defined well used trails. While hiking, it was easy to space out and daydream. On the Continental Divide Trail I had to stay focused. It took way too long to get that through my thick skull. Before starting my CDT hike I had been given the same advice many times. "The CDT is tricky. You will think you are on the Trail and you won't be. Check your map and GPS often." I believed the advice givers. I was going to follow the advice.

Right from the start I got burned over and over. I would be following a dirt road and there didn't seem to be any other options but to follow the road. Since I didn't see any options I would hike miles without checking my GPS. When I finally did check I was way off course. Grrr! In the early days of my hike I would set off cross country to get back on course. Too many times I reached my waypoint dusty and full of scratches. After a while I would just turn around and head back to where I made my mistake. Often the turnoff would be a little unmarked pathway next to the road. Sometimes it would be marked and I wasn't paying attention. Other times the CDT would leave the road and head cross country. Time after time I would let my guard down and time after time I would get burned. By Cuba, New Mexico I was finally doing what I should have been doing from the start. I would automatically check my GPS every fifteen minutes. If there was even the slightest doubt in my mind that I was still on the Trail I would check the GPS.

Lesson learned: Check the GPS every fifteen minutes no matter what. If in doubt check the GPS.

Equipment

This equipment works for me:

Boots: I used Keen Targhee ll boots hiking the Continental Divide Trail and didn't have any problems with blisters. I like them. They give my feet good support and are comfortable. I like their wide toe box. I used trail runners on my Pacific Crest Trail hike and prefer the Keens. There were more small rocks in the New Mexico desert than I was expecting and the Keens cruised right over them. They have excellent grip going downhill. My boots were two sizes larger than my normal shoe size. They are so comfortable I wear them when I am not hiking.

Socks: I used two pair of Darn Tough socks on my hike - one for sleeping and one for hiking. I wish I had known about these socks when I was hiking the Appalachian Trail and Pacific Crest Trail. I wore out many pair of socks on those hikes. The Darn Tough socks were comfortable from the first time I put them on. I crossed the Gila River over 200 times and they fit smoothly on my feet even when I was wading through water. They hold their form and never bunch. I still use them every day. The socks I hiked with on the Continental Divide Trail now have over 1,000 miles of use and many miles still left in them. I thought they might be too warm when I was hiking in the desert heat but they weren't. They have a lifetime guarantee.

Dirty Girl Gators: They are so light I thought they might be fragile. They were as tough as nails and kept the desert sand, little gritty pebbles, and dirt out of my boots. It was a pleasure not having to stop and take pebbles out of my boots while hiking. When I removed my boots at night there wasn't any dirt or sand in them. They kept my socks clean, too. On the Pacific Crest Trail I didn't use gators. When I emptied my shoes at night there would be a little pile of dirt at the foot of the tent. Shaking my socks out created a thirty second dust cloud.

My feet were healthy and blister-free for the duration of my CDT hike. My Dirty Girl Gators kept the dirt and grit out of my boots, my Darn Tough socks fit smoothly on my feet and stayed that way throughout the day, and my Keen Targhee ll boots with the wide toe box were comfortable and gave my feet the support they needed.

Sleeping Bag: I finally splurged and bought a good lightweight down sleeping bag for my CDT hike. I wish I had made that decision before hiking the AT and PCT. I slept better with the down bag. On cold nights it stayed closer to its rating than the synthetic bag.

Air Mattress: I started hiking the Appalachian Trail with a sleeping pad. It was light as a feather but I could feel everything underneath me. The hard shelter floors made me groan. By Hot Springs, North Carolina I replaced the sleeping pad with an air mattress. It was like night and day. I slept much better.

Hiking Stick: I used sturdy hiking poles on the Appalachian Trail and they did a great job. On the Pacific Crest Trail I broke a hiking pole less than one hundred miles into the hike. The nearest town didn't have hiking poles for sale but they did have hiking sticks. I bought one planning to get some new hiking poles once I reached a town big enough to sell them. I really liked the hiking stick. It gave me the stability I needed and freed up one hand to swat horse flies or eat food while I was hiking. By the time I reached Canada I had worn almost two inches off of the stick. I bought a thicker, sturdier hickory hiking stick for my CDT hike and couldn't be happier with it.

Marmot Driclime Windshirt: I love this jacket. I bought it in 2011 and have used it every spring, winter, and fall since. The inside is soft and comfortable and the outside repels wind beautifully. On the PCT and CDT it was my go-to jacket once I reached camp.

Sawyer Squeeze Filter & Aqua Mira Drops: The Sawyer Squeeze Filter works fast and effectively. I filtered filthy cow tank water with it and the water came out sparkling clean. I used the Aqua Mira Drops when needed on the Pacific Crest Trail and to make double sure on filtered cow tank water on the Continental Divide Trail.

12 CONCLUSION

My first backpacking adventure was in 1973 when I hiked the Shenandoah section of the Appalachian Trail. Unintentionally, I did a lot of things to keep my pack light which, unintentionally again, made my hike more enjoyable. I borrowed a down sleeping bag. I planned to sleep in shelters so I didn't take a tent. I ate freeze dried food and had a small external frame pack so I couldn't load it up.

I didn't know any better and wore blue jeans, a white cotton tee shirt, and the mesh boots I had worn in Vietnam. I was outdoors breathing the fresh mountain air, pushing my body up mountains, and feeling fit and strong. At night I socialized with other hikers around the campfire. I really enjoyed that ten day hike. It was a good introduction to backpacking.

Through the years I continued backpacking in many of the mountain ranges of New Mexico and parts of Arizona. In 1985 I spent a month in the Gila Mountains and saw only five people the whole time. Backpacking was a great way to enjoy nature, relax, and get away from it all.

From the very beginning one of my goals was to thru-hike the Appalachian Trail. I was finally able to do that at age sixty-two. The physical and mental challenge was enormous but the feeling of accomplishment at its completion was indescribable. Thru-hiking turned out to be even more enjoyable than I imagined. After thru-hiking the Appalachian Trail I knew the Pacific Crest Trail was next. There were fewer people on the Pacific Crest Trail and I spent more time alone. I loved it. Some of my best memories are of nights alone under the stars listening to the mournful howl of a coyote or the soft hoot of an owl. After hiking the Pacific Crest Trail I had to try for the Triple Crown. To complete the Triple Crown I needed to hike the Continental Divide Trail. I hiked 980 miles of the Continental Divide Trail before realizing I had stalled too long waiting for the snow to melt in the San Juan Mountains and wouldn't make it to Canada before the snows blocked the Trail. I was disappointed but hiking as far as I did allowed me to clearly define how I want to hike the Continental Divide Trail in 2016. I am already starting to physically and mentally prepare for that hike.

Thru-hiking has provided me with an entertaining way to spend my retirement. I enjoy the preparation for each hike, the anticipation before a hike, and the physical and mental challenges while hiking. With experience has come increased confidence. I like the feeling of continuing to grow as I age.

I am eagerly looking forward to thru-hiking the Continental Divide Trail in 2016. For the past six months I have averaged a little over six miles a day walking and will continue to do so until I start my hike. I can already feel the mental focus I had on my Appalachian Trail and Pacific Crest Trail thru-hikes starting to come into play. I'm ready to get this show on the road! I can't wait!

ABOUT THE AUTHOR

Jim Hill is an avid backpacker who has thru-hiked the Appalachian Trail and Pacific Crest Trail. He has written books about those adventures: "Are You Ready To Hike The Pacific Crest Trail?" and "Appalachian Adventure". He lives in Rio Rancho, New Mexico.

Made in the USA
San Bernardino, CA
27 November 2015